NATIONAL
GEOGRAPHIC
KiDS

AWESOME
Maths &
English
AGE 5-7

Get awesome at Maths and English!

Explore some of the world's most amazing animals and exercise brain cells on the way!

Four wild adventures open up fascinating facts about different creatures and provide practice for Maths and English:

- Gaze at animals found in **grasslands** while going through the **Maths** topics for **Ages 5–6**.

- Marvel at **rainforest creatures** while roaming through the **Maths** topics for **Ages 6–7**.

- Admire animals that can be found in **Asia** while advancing through the **Phonics and Spelling** topics.

- Uncover creatures that live in, on or by the **sea** while navigating the **Grammar and Punctuation** topics.

Awesome adventures await… good luck, explorer!

Published by Collins
An imprint of HarperCollins*Publishers*
Westerhill Road
Bishopbriggs
Glasgow G64 2QT

In association with National Geographic Partners, LLC

NATIONAL GEOGRAPHIC and the Yellow Border Design are trademarks of the National Geographic Society, used under license.

First published 2020

Text copyright © 2020 HarperCollins*Publishers*. All Rights Reserved.

Design copyright © 2020 National Geographic Partners, LLC. All Rights Reserved.

ISBN: 978-0-00-838880-5

10 9 8 7 6 5 4 3 2

A catalogue record for this book is available from the British Library

Printed and bound in China by RR Donnelley APS

If you would like to comment on any aspect of this book, please contact us at the above address or online.

natgeokidsbooks.co.uk

collins.reference@harpercollins.co.uk

Acknowledgements

P5, 46, 115 © B. G Thomson/Science Photo Library; P55, Buiten-Beeld / Alamy; P79, Natural Visions /Alamy. All other images are ©Shutterstock.com and ©HarperCollins*Publishers*

Publisher: Michelle I'Anson
Authors: Alan Dobbs, Frances Naismith, Jill Atkins and Shelley Welsh
Project Manager: Richard Toms
Cover Design: Sarah Duxbury
Inside Concept Design: Ian Wrigley
Page Layout: Ian Wrigley and Rose and Thorn Creative Services Ltd

Features of this book

Practice Tasks – activities to build confidence and improve skills

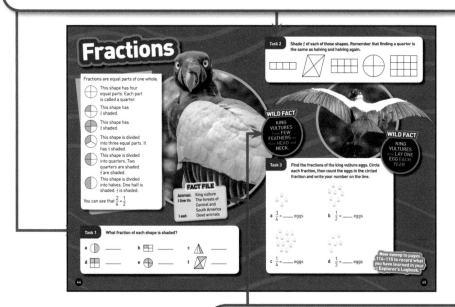

Wild Facts and Fact Files – weird, funny and interesting animal facts

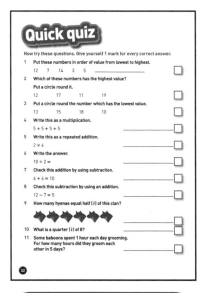

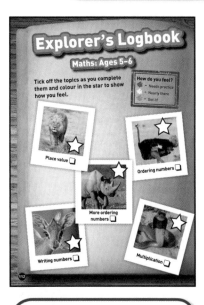

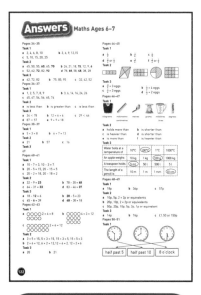

Quick Quizzes – more activities to recap skills and understanding

Explorer's Logbook – a tracker to record progress

Answers – the solutions to all the activities are at the back of the book

A certificate (see back page) rewards completion of the book.

Contents

Maths: Ages 5–6

Maths: Ages 6–7

Phonics and Spelling: Ages 5–7

Grammar and Punctuation: Ages 5–7

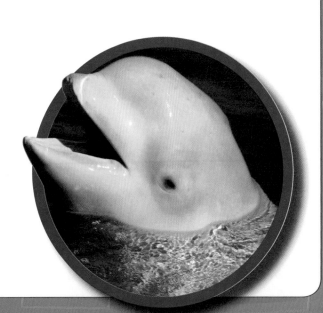

Place value

All numbers are made from the digits **1, 2, 3, 4, 5, 6, 7, 8, 9** and **0** (zero).

If it is a single-digit number, then it has to be **0, 1, 2, 3, 4, 5, 6, 7, 8** or **9**.

In a two-digit number, like 23, the 2 has a value of 20 and the 3 is worth three ones. The 2 has a higher value than the 3 because of its place in the number.

A zero is used as a place holder. The number 10 has a zero to show 1 lot of ten and 0 ones.

An abacus can show numbers with different values. It uses beads to show each digit.

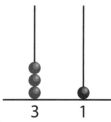

| 3 | 1 |

This abacus shows 3 lots of ten and 1 lot of one.

The number is 31.

WILD FACT

The **FEMALE LIONS,** called **LIONESSES,** do most of the **HUNTING** for the **PRIDE.**

Task 1

Write each of these numbers, using the abacus beads to help you.

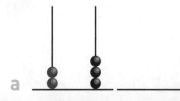

a _____

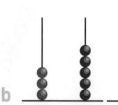

b _____

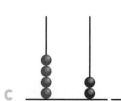

c _____

Task 2 Look at the single-digit numbers on the lions below.

1 2 3 4

a Use two of the single-digit numbers to make a two-digit number. _____

b Use two of the numbers to make the highest value two-digit number that you can. _____

c Now use two of the numbers to make the lowest value two-digit number that you can. _____

Task 3 Write down the value of the underlined digit. The first two have been done for you.

2<u>1</u>   1

<u>4</u>6   40

a 3<u>6</u> _____

b <u>2</u>4 _____

c 5<u>7</u> _____

d <u>7</u>3 _____

e <u>4</u>5 _____

f <u>9</u>9 _____

LIONS are the only wild cats that **LIVE TOGETHER.** A group of lions is called a **PRIDE.**

Now look for pages 112–113 and fill in your Explorer's Logbook.

Ordering numbers

Understanding the **place** that a digit has and which numbers would be **one more** and **one less** helps you to put numbers in **order**.

If the number is 12, then one more would be 13 and one less would be 11.

On a number line, it would look like this:

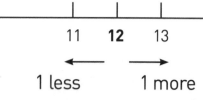

11   **12**   13

← 1 less   1 more →

WILD FACT

The **OSTRICH** is the **LARGEST BIRD IN THE WORLD.** It has very strong legs and can run at 70 km/h (43 mph).

Task 1   Count the ostriches and write one more and one less of each set.

a One less _____   One more _____

b One less _____   One more _____

c One less _____   One more _____

Use the number line to answer these questions.

| | | | | | | | | | | | | | | | | | |
|13|14|15|16|17|18|19|20|21|22|23|24|25|26|27|28|29|30|

a Write the number that is one less than 16.   _____

b Which number is one more than 29?   _____

c Write the number that is one less than 24.   _____

d Which number is one more than 13?   _____

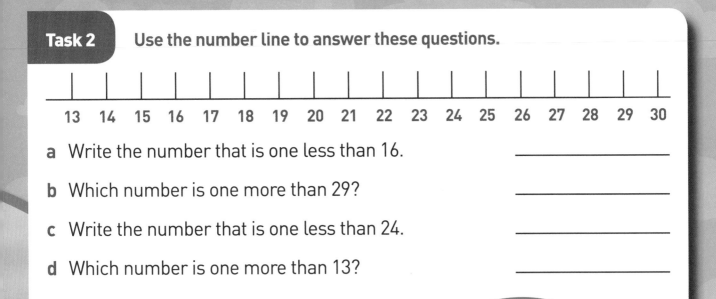

Task 3   Complete the grid to show one more and one less for each number shown.

One less		One more
	56	
	34	
	21	
	2	
	13	
	73	
	55	

WILD FACT

OSTRICHES have the **LARGEST EYEBALLS** of any bird. Each eyeball is **BIGGER** than its brain!

Now sprint to pages 112–113 and fill in your Explorer's Logbook.

More ordering numbers

Look at these numbers:
12   7   23

If they were in **order**, the numbers would look like this:
7   12   23
(**7** is the **lowest** and **23** is the **highest**).

Numbers can be ordered in different ways. The numbers below go from **highest** to **lowest**. They are still in an order, but the order is different.

12   8   5   3   1

FACT FILE

Animal: Black rhinoceros
I live in: African grassland, woodland and wetland
I weigh: Up to 1400 kg
I eat: Leaves and fruit from trees and bushes

WILD FACT

BLACK RHINOCEROS enjoy rolling in MUD, as it helps them to KEEP COOL and protects them from the sun.

Task 1

Put these numbers in order from lowest to highest.

a   14   26   3   32   12   _____

b   45   13   7   2   29   _____

c   16   3   23   21   60   _____

d   54   43   10   51   13   _____

Put these numbers in order from highest to lowest.

a   2   10   6   8   3

_____

b   16   20   4   34   18

_____

c   5   27   16   39   51

_____

Task 3 One of these lines has numbers that are lowest to highest. Put a tick in the box for this line.

5	9	3	10	12	☐
12	14	16	18	20	☐
10	7	4	3	1	☐

WILD FACT

The **RHINOCEROS' HORN** is extremely strong. It contains **KERATIN,** which is what your hair and nails are made of.

Task 4 This line is counting from lowest to highest. Insert the missing numbers.

2 ☐ 4 ☐ 6 ☐

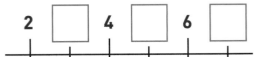

Now charge over to pages 112–113 and fill in your Explorer's Logbook.

Writing numbers

Numbers can be written as **numerals** (figures).

Numbers can also be written as **words**.

For example, **one**, **two** and **three** are numbers written as words, and the number **10** written as a word is **ten**.

FACT FILE

Animal:	Dik-dik
I live in:	African savannah, woodland and grassland
I weigh:	Up to 6 kg
I eat:	Plants, leaves and fruit

WILD FACT

DIK-DIKS DON'T NEED to **DRINK WATER.** They can get all their fluids from the food they eat.

Task 1	Write these numbers as words.

a 8 _____

b 6 _____

c 12 _____

d 3 _____

Task 2

Write these words as numerals.

a five _____

b twenty _____

c eleven _____

d one _____

Task 3

Draw lines to match the words to their numerals.

sixteen   9

seven   8

nine   16

eight   7

WILD FACT

DIK-DIKS sometimes STAND on their back legs to reach LEAVES AND FRUIT.

Task 4

Look at the numerals, then fill in the blanks to complete the words.

a 7 ____e____e____

b 14 f____u____t____e____

c 21 tw____n____y-____n____

d 43 ____o____ty-t____r____e

Now spring to pages 112–113 and fill in your Explorer's Logbook.

Multiplication

Numbers can be counted in different ways. Multiplication is the same as repeated addition.

2 × 3 is **3 lots of 2**, which is the same as **2 + 2 + 2**. 2 × 3 can also mean **2 lots of 3**, which is the same as **3 + 3**. The answer for each calculation is **6**.

WILD FACT

When defending itself, a **CAPE COBRA** will **RAISE ITS BODY** high into the air, **HISS** and unfold the flaps of skin on either side of its head, known as its **HOOD.**

FACT FILE

Animal:	Cape cobra
I live in:	Deserts and savannah in the far south of Africa
I am:	Up to 1.5 metres long
I eat:	Small mammals, lizards, birds and eggs

Task 1

Write each multiplication as a repeated addition. An example has been done for you.

2 × 4 =   <u>2</u> + <u>2</u> + <u>2</u> + <u>2</u> **or** <u>4</u> + <u>4</u>

a 5 × 3 = _____

b 10 × 5 = _____

c 2 × 6 = _____

Task 2 Write these additions as multiplications. An example has been done for you.

$5 + 5 + 5 = \underline{5} \times \underline{3} \text{ or } \underline{3} \times \underline{5}$

a $10 + 10 + 10 + 10 + 10 =$ _____

b $2 + 2 + 2 + 2 + 2 + 2 + 2 =$ _____

c $5 + 5 + 5 + 5 + 5 + 5 + 5 =$ _____

WILD FACT

CAPE COBRAS have a TOXIC BITE that can KILL a person within 30 minutes.

Task 3 Write the answers to these multiplications. An example has been done for you.

$5 \times 2 = 10$

a $2 \times 5 =$ _____

b $10 \times 6 =$ _____

c $2 \times 8 =$ _____

Task 4 Fill in the correct numbers to complete these multiplications.

a $3 \times$ ___ $= 15$

b ___ $\times 2 = 12$

c $4 \times$ ___ $= 16$

d ___ $\times 3 = 18$

Now slither over to pages 112–113 and fill in your Explorer's Logbook.

Division

WILD FACT

The **STRIPED COAT** makes it more difficult for a lion or other predator to pick out an individual **ZEBRA** in a **LARGE GROUP.**

Dividing a number means **sharing** it into **equal amounts**. If you share 10 apples between 2 children, each child would get 5 apples. The calculation would look like this:

$10 \div 2 = 5$

You can find out other facts by dividing a group by 2.

If you know that **$6 \div 2 = 3$** then you also know that there are **3 groups of 2 in 6!**

FACT FILE

Animal:	Zebra
I live in:	African grassland
I weigh:	Up to 450 kg
I eat:	Grass

Task 1 Divide these clumps of grass between two zebras. Write the calculation in each case. An example has been done for you.

 $6 \div 2 = 3$

a _____

b _____

c _____

d  _____

Task 2 Look at the zebras and write down the division calculation and the answer.

 = _____

Task 3 How many sets of two are there in the groups of zebras?

a  = _____ sets of two.

b 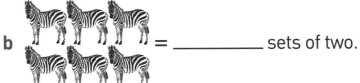 = _____ sets of two.

c  = _____ sets of two.

Now gallop to pages 112–113 and fill in your Explorer's Logbook.

Checking your maths

Addition (**+**) is the opposite of subtraction (**−**) and multiplication (**×**) is the opposite of division (**÷**).

You can check your addition calculations by using subtraction and you can check your multiplication calculations using division (and the other way round).

2 + 4 = 6 and **6 − 4 = 2**

Can you see that they are the opposite to each other?

FACT FILE

Animal:	Spotted hyena
I live in:	African woodland, grassland and savannah
I weigh:	Up to 85 kg
I eat:	Wildebeest, antelopes, and the leftovers of other animals

Task 1 Look at these additions and do the opposite subtraction. An example has been done for you.

$$5 + 3 = 8 \qquad 8 - 3 = 5$$

a $2 + 1 = 3$ _____

b $6 + 1 = 7$ _____

c $4 + 6 = 10$ _____

Task 2   Now write these multiplications as the opposite division. An example has been done for you.

$2 \times 5 = 10$ $10 \div 5 = 2$

a $3 \times 2 = 6$ _____

b $4 \times 2 = 8$ _____

c $6 \times 2 = 12$ _____

d $2 \times 10 = 20$ _____

WILD FACT

HYENAS live in **LARGE GROUPS** of up to 130 animals, known as **'CLANS'**. They communicate with each other by 'whooping', which sounds as if they are laughing!

WILD FACT

HYENAS have **POWERFUL JAWS** to break through the **TOUGHEST SKIN AND BONE.** They can even digest bone.

Task 3   Write the opposite of these calculations. An example has been done for you.

$10 \times 2 = 20$ $20 \div 2 = 10$

a $2 + 10 = 12$ _____

b $10 \div 2 = 5$ _____

c $20 - 10 = 10$ _____

Now take your clan to pages 112–113 and fill in your Explorer's Logbook.

Fractions

Fractions are equal parts of one whole.

This circle has been split into **two equal parts**. Each part is one **half**, or $\frac{1}{2}$. One half is shaded.

This circle has been split into **four equal parts**. Each part is a **quarter**, or $\frac{1}{4}$. One quarter is shaded.

Groups can also be split into halves ($\frac{1}{2}$). In this group of four bush babies, half ($\frac{1}{2}$) would be two bush babies.

(Remember that two halves have equal value.)

Splitting into quarters is the same as halving and halving again. To split a group into quarters ($\frac{1}{4}$), there must be four equal parts. If you first split the group in half, and split each half in half again, you have four equal quarters.

| Task 1 | Colour the correct fractions of each circle. |

a $\frac{1}{2}$

b $\frac{1}{4}$

Task 2 Write the number that is half ($\frac{1}{2}$) of these groups of bush babies.

a  $\frac{1}{2}$ = _____

b $\frac{1}{2}$ = _____

c $\frac{1}{2}$ = _____

WILD FACT

BUSH BABIES are small, but noisy! They make loud, HIGH-PITCHED SOUNDS, which sound very like a HUMAN BABY.

WILD FACT

When HUNTING, BUSH BABIES fold back their big ears so that they don't get in the way as they LEAP from TREE TO TREE.

Task 3 Find a quarter ($\frac{1}{4}$) of these groups of bush babies.

a $\frac{1}{4}$ = _____

b $\frac{1}{4}$ = _____

c $\frac{1}{4}$ = _____

Now climb to pages 112–113 and fill in your Explorer's Logbook.

Measuring

You can measure lots of things in lots of ways. **Length** (how long something is) and **height** (how tall something is) are measured in centimetres (cm) and metres (m). **Mass** or **weight** (how heavy something is) is measured using grams (g) and kilograms (kg). **Capacity** (how much something holds) is measured using millilitres (ml) and litres (l).

WILD FACT

GIRAFFES are the **TALLEST ANIMALS** in the world. Surprisingly, their long necks only have **7 BONES** – the same number as you!

FACT FILE

Animal: Giraffe
I live in: Grasslands and woodlands of Africa
I am: Up to 6 metres tall
I eat: Leaves and plants

Task 1

Look at this giraffe. It measures 4 metres (4 m). It is 4 m tall, or 4 m in height.

A

Now look at this giraffe. It measures 3 metres (3 m). It is 3 m tall, or 3 m in height.

B

Which giraffe is taller, **A** or **B**?

_____

Giraffes eat lots of leaves. Each symbol  represents 1 kg of leaves.

Giraffe **A** eats this amount:

Giraffe **B** eats this amount:

a How many kilograms of leaves does each giraffe eat?

Giraffe **A** _____

Giraffe **B** _____

b Which giraffe eats more, **A** or **B**?

_____

WILD FACT

To take a **DRINK, GIRAFFES** have to do the **SPLITS!**

Task 3

Each symbol represents 1 litre of water.

Giraffe **A** drank this many litres of water:

Giraffe **B** drank this many litres of water:

a How much water did each giraffe drink?

Giraffe **A** _____

Giraffe **B** _____

b Which giraffe drank less?

_____

Now stride to pages 112–113 and fill in your Explorer's Logbook.

Understanding time

Time is measured in **seconds**, **minutes** and **hours**.

1 minute = 60 seconds, and 1 hour = 60 minutes.

The **short hand** on a clock face tells you what hour it is.

The **long hand** tells you how many minutes to or past the hour it is.

Longer units of time include **days**, **months** and **years**. 7 days is equal to 1 **week**. 4 weeks is approximately 1 month and there are 12 months in a year.

When the **long hand** is pointing at 12 and the **short hand** points to a number, this is **o'clock**.
The time on this clock is 5 o'clock.

When the **long hand** is pointing at 6 and the **short hand** is halfway between two numbers, the time is **half past the hour**. The short hand on this clock is between 8 and 9, so it is showing a time of half past 8.

Task 1 Draw the hands on these clocks to show the following times that the baboons took a rest.

a 3 o'clock   **b** 10 o'clock   **c** 2 o'clock

Task 2 Draw the hands on these clocks to show the times that the baboons were grooming.

a Half past 7   **b** Half past 9   **c** Half past 4

WILD FACT

BABOONS spend hours **GROOMING EACH OTHER**, which helps them to make and **KEEP FRIENDS.**

Task 3 Answer these.

a Baby baboons can spend their first two months clinging to their mothers. Approximately how many weeks is this?

_____ weeks

b Show how you worked this out:

_____

_____

Now walk over to pages 112–113 and fill in your Explorer's Logbook.

2D and 3D shapes

There are two main kinds of **shape**: **flat** or two-dimensional (**2D**) shapes and **solid** or three-dimensional (**3D**) shapes.

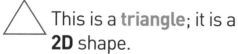 This is a **triangle**; it is a **2D** shape.

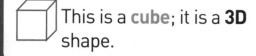 This is a **cube**; it is a **3D** shape.

FACT FILE

Animal:	African elephant
I live in:	Grassland and savannah of Africa
I am:	Up to 4 metres tall
I eat:	Shrubs, grasses, roots and fruit

Task 1

Look at these 2D shapes. Draw a line to match the shape to its name. One has been done for you.

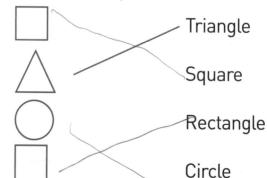

Triangle

Square

Rectangle

Circle

Task 2

Using the names in the box, write the name of the 3D shape next to its picture.

cylinder   cuboid   cone   pyramid

a   Cuboid

b   Cylinder

c   Cone

d   ✓ p

WILD FACT

ELEPHANTS use their **TRUNKS** in **LOTS OF WAYS.** They use them for smelling, for moving food and water to their mouth and even as a snorkel to breathe through when they cross deep rivers!

Task 3

Are these shapes 2D or 3D? Tick the correct box for each one.

	2D	3D
△	✓	
cylinder		✓
octagon	✓	
cuboid		✓

WILD FACT

AFRICAN ELEPHANTS are the **LARGEST LAND ANIMAL** on Earth. They can weigh **UP TO 6300 KG!**

Now lumber to pages 112–113 and fill in your Explorer's Logbook.

29

Money

Money is used to pay for things.

Money can be either coins or notes. The different coins and notes each have their own value.

We use the letter 'p' to represent **pence** and the symbol '£' to represent **pounds**.

FACT FILE

Animal: Honey badger
I live in: Deserts, grasslands and woodlands of Africa and Asia
I weigh: Up to 14 kg
I eat: Honey, insects, fruit and small animals

Task 1 Each jar of honey costs 2p. How much would you have to pay for these jars of honey?

a = _____6_____ p

b = _____10_____ p

c = _____12_____ p

Task 2 A large pot of honey costs 10p. Here are some of the coins that can be used to pay for the honey. The coins all have different values.

Write three different ways of making 10p from the coins above. You can use any combination of the coins. You can use more than one coin of the same value.

$\times$ 5p _____ = 10p

$\times$ 5 - 2p _____ = 10p

$\times$ 10 - 1p _____ = 10p

Task 3 Here are some coins.

£2   £1   20p   50p

a Put the coins in order from lowest value to highest value.

Lowest _____ **Highest**

b How many 2p coins would have the same value as one 10p coin?

_____

c How many 10p coins would have the same value as one 50p coin?

_____

Now scurry to pages 112–113 and fill in your Explorer's Logbook.

Quick quiz

Now try these questions. Give yourself 1 mark for every correct answer.

1   Put these numbers in order of value from lowest to highest.

12   7   14   3   5   _3 5 7 12 14_   ☑

2   Which of these numbers has the highest value?

Put a circle round it.

12   17   11   ⟨19⟩   ☐

3   Put a circle round the number which has the lowest value.

13   15   18   ⟨10⟩   ☐

4   Write this as a multiplication.

$5 + 5 + 5 + 5$ _5 × 4 = 20_   ☐

5   Write this as a repeated addition.

2×4 _____   ☐

6   Write the answer.

$10 \div 2 =$ _____   ☐

7   Check this addition by using subtraction.

$6 + 4 = 10$ _____   ☐

8   Check this subtraction by using an addition.

$12 - 7 = 5$ _____   ☐

9   How many hyenas equal half ($\frac{1}{2}$) of this clan?

_____   ☐

10   What is a quarter ($\frac{1}{4}$) of 8?   _____   ☐

11   Some baboons spent 1 hour each day grooming.
For how many hours did they groom each
other in 5 days?   _____   ☐

12 Put these weights in order from lightest to heaviest.

12kg   1kg   10kg   3kg   _____

13 Here is a clock face showing the time now. 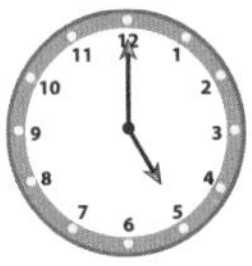
         What time will it be in 1 hour? Draw the hands on the clock.

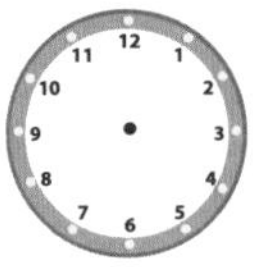

14 Which of these shapes is NOT a triangle?

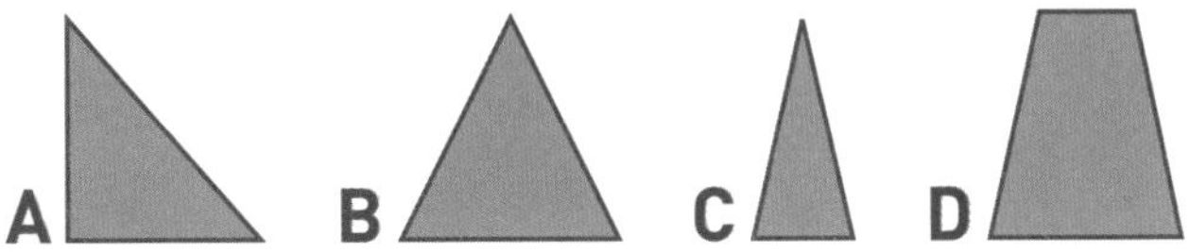

A   B   C   D   _____

15 What is the name of this 3D shape?

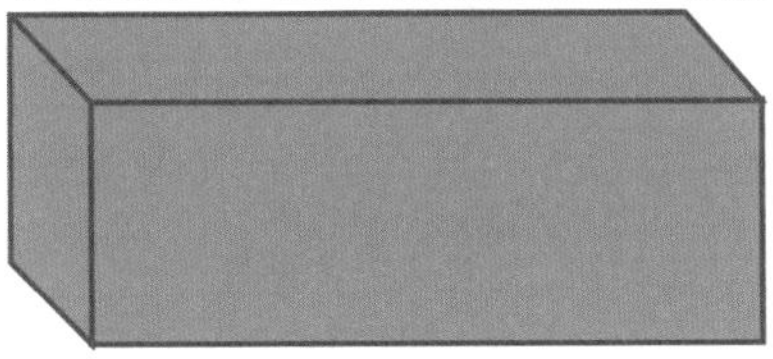

_____

16 Which shape is the odd one out? Tick the correct box.

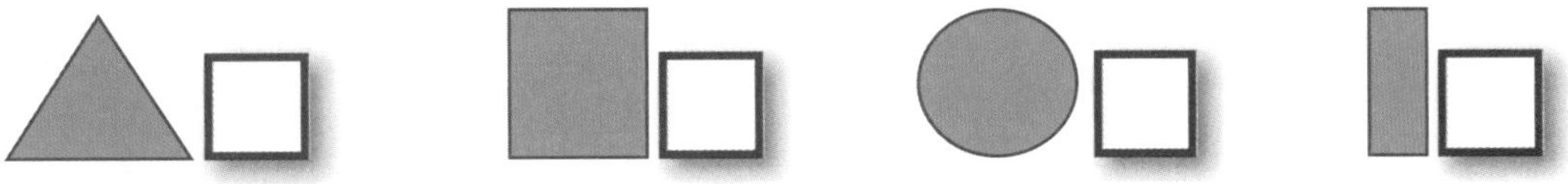

17 Why did you choose the shape that you ticked in question 16?

_____

18 Which of the coins shown below has the highest value?

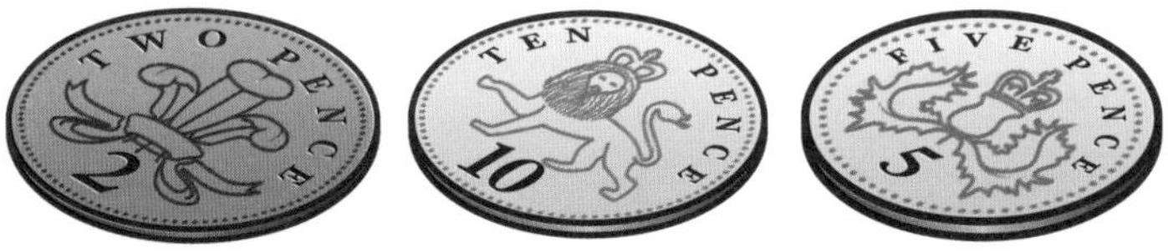

_____

19 Which of the coins shown above has the lowest value?

_____

20 What is the total of all of the coins shown above?

_____

Counting

You can hop along a number line, just like a frog!

For example, you can count on or back in steps of 2, 3 or 5, like this:

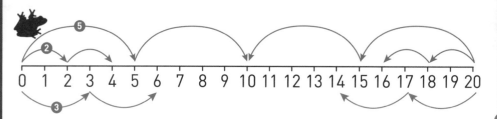

You can also count from any number in tens.

When you count **on** in tens, **you add 10 each time** and **the ones digit stays the same**.

For example:

26, 36, 46, 56...   the 'tens' digit goes up by 1
                     the 'ones' digit stays the same

When you count **back** in tens, **the tens digit goes down by 1 each time** and **the ones digit stays the same**.

For example: **67, 57, 47, 37...**

WILD FACT

The **RED-EYED TREE FROG** also has **BLUE STREAKS** and **ORANGE TOES.** These warn off animals that might want to eat it.

WILD FACT

The **RED-EYED TREE FROG CLOSES ITS BRIGHT EYES** and **COVERS UP ITS COLOURS WHEN SLEEPING,** to avoid being seen.

Task 1

Use the number line to count on.

```
0  1  2  3  4  5  6  7  8  9  10 11 12 13 14 15 16 17 18 19 20 21 22 23 24 25 26 27 28 29 30
```

a Count on from zero in steps of 2.

What are the first five numbers? _____ _____ _____ _____ _____

b Count on from zero in steps of 3.

What are the first five numbers? _____ _____ _____ _____ _____

c Count on from zero in steps of 5.

What are the first five numbers? _____ _____ _____ _____ _____

Task 2

Help the red-eyed tree frog to fill in the missing numbers in each sequence.

Use the 100 square to help you.

a 45   50   55   ____   65   ____

b 24   21   18   ____   12   9   ____

c 52   62   ____   82   ____

d 78   ____   58   ____   38   28

1	2	3	4	5	6	7	8	9	10
11	12	13	14	15	16	17	18	19	20
21	22	23	24	25	26	27	28	29	30
31	32	33	34	35	36	37	38	39	40
41	42	43	44	45	46	47	48	49	50
51	52	53	54	55	56	57	58	59	60
61	62	63	64	65	66	67	68	69	70
71	72	73	74	75	76	77	78	79	80
81	82	83	84	85	86	87	88	89	90
91	92	93	94	95	96	97	98	99	100

Task 3

Count on in tens. Write the next three numbers in the sequences.

a 33   43   53

_____ _____ _____

b 45   55   65

_____ _____ _____

c 2   12   22

_____ _____ _____

Now spring to pages 114–115 to record what you have learned in your Explorer's Logbook.

Compare and order numbers

You can compare numbers and put them in order by looking at the place value of the digits.

Example: Which is greater, 23 or 21?

Both numbers have 2 tens so look at the ones.

2**3** is greater because it has **3** ones; 2**1** only has **1** one.

So 23 is greater than 21.

These symbols are used in maths:

- $>$ means 'is greater than'. So $5 > 2$ means 5 **is greater than** 2.
- $<$ means 'is less than'. So $4 < 8$ means 4 **is less than** 8.
- $=$ means 'is equal to'. So $2 = 1 + 1$ means 2 **is equal to** 1 plus 1.

WILD FACT

The **HOWLER MONKEY'S CALLS** are **VERY LOUD** and can be heard up to **5 KM (3 MILES) AWAY!**

Task 1

Put these numbers in order from smallest to largest.

a 5   9   2   7   1   8

_____

b 14   6   26   3   16   24

_____

c 45 54 74 65 47 56

_____

WILD FACT

HOWLER MONKEYS' TAILS can CURL AROUND and GRIP BRANCHES – just like an extra hand!

Task 2

The howler monkeys have found some number cards. Write the symbol 'is greater than' or 'is less than' between each pair of numbers.

a _____   **b** _____   **c** _____

Task 3

Each of these three monkeys has a symbol:

Write one of the symbols in the orange box between these number pairs and sums.

a 34 ☐ 78

b 12 ☐ 6 + 6

c 29 ☐ 46

d 87 ☐ 57

e 9 + 9 ☐ 18

f 1 ☐ 0

Now swing to pages 114–115 to record what you have learned in your Explorer's Logbook.

Add numbers

The symbol for adding is +

All these words mean add: together more count on plus sum total

Number bonds are the two numbers you need to add together to make another number.

You need to learn all the number bonds to 10 and 20.

Number bonds to 10			Number bonds to 20			
0 + 10	4 + 6	7 + 3	0 + 20	5 + 15	10 + 10	15 + 5
1 + 9	5 + 5	8 + 2	1 + 19	6 + 14	11 + 9	16 + 4
2 + 8	6 + 4	9 + 1	2 + 18	7 + 13	12 + 8	17 + 3
3 + 7		10 + 0	3 + 17	8 + 12	13 + 7	18 + 2
			4 + 16	9 + 11	14 + 6	19 + 1
						20 + 0

You can use a **number line** to help to count **on**.

For example: 14 + 9

Put your finger at 14 on the number line.

Count on 9 places.

0 1 2 3 4 5 6 7 8 9 10 11 12 13 14 15 16 17 18 19 20 21 22 23 24 25 26 27 28 29 30

14 + 9 = 23

You can add numbers in any order:

2 + 3 = 5 and 3 + 2 = 5

Try it on the number line!

You can also **partition numbers** to help to add them.

15 + 24 = 15 + 20 + 4 = 39

Task 1 Count the ants and write the correct numbers on the lines. The first one has been done for you.

🐜🐜🐜🐜 + 🐜🐜 =

$\underline{\quad 4 \quad}$ $\underline{\quad 2 \quad}$ $\underline{\quad 6 \quad}$

🐜🐜🐜🐜 + 🐜🐜🐜 =

a _____ _____ _____

🐜🐜🐜🐜🐜 + 🐜🐜🐜🐜🐜🐜🐜 =

b _____ _____ _____

Task 2 Write the answers to these addition problems.

a $13 + 8 =$ _____

b $27 + 30 =$ _____

c $5 + 7 + 4 =$ _____

Task 3 A giant anteater eats 23 ants. It then scoops up another 46 ants. How many ants is that altogether?

_____

Now flick out your tongue and stroll to pages 114–115 to record what you have learned in your Explorer's Logbook.

Subtract numbers

The symbol for subtracting is —

All these words mean subtract: take away   count back   left over   less   minus

From your number bonds, you know that 12 + 8 = 20 and 8 + 12 = 20.

You can use these number bonds to make some subtraction facts.

20 − 8 = 12 and 20 − 12 = 8

(Remember that you cannot subtract a larger number from a smaller one.)

You can use a **number line** to count **back**.

Look at this example: 17 − 12

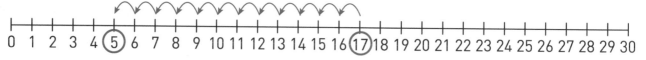

17 − 12 = 5

You can also use a **100 square** to count back.

Look at this example: 47 – 28

1	2	3	4	5	6	7	8	9	10
11	12	13	14	15	16	17	18	19	20
21	22	23	24	25	26	27	28	29	30
31	32	33	34	35	36	37	38	39	40
41	42	43	44	45	46	47	48	49	50
51	52	53	54	55	56	57	58	59	60
61	62	63	64	65	66	67	68	69	70
71	72	73	74	75	76	77	78	79	80
81	82	83	84	85	86	87	88	89	90
91	92	93	94	95	96	97	98	99	100

Count back two lots of 10 (20), then count back another 8.

47 – 20 – 8

47 – 28 = 19

FACT FILE

Animal: Rainbow boa

I live in: Tropical forests of Central and South America

I eat: Small animals and birds

Task 1 Write two subtraction facts for each of these addition facts. An example has been done for you.

$6 + 4 = 10$ $10 - 6 = 4$ $10 - 4 = 6$

a $3 + 7 = 10$ _____ _____

b $15 + 5 = 20$ _____ _____

c $18 + 2 = 20$ _____ _____

Task 2 Use a number line or a 100 square to find the answers.

a $32 - 9 =$ _____

b $78 - 30 =$ _____

c $64 - 31 =$ _____

d $83 - 46 =$ _____

Task 3 Fill in the missing numbers.

a $18 - \boxed{} = 6$ b $\boxed{} - 5 = 23$

c $45 - \boxed{} = 39$ d $\boxed{} - 30 = 18$

Now slither to pages 114–115 to record what you have learned in your Explorer's Logbook.

Multiply and divide

Here are 12 Komodo dragon eggs:

You can look at them as arrays of:

3 lots of 4   or   **4 lots of 3**

$3 \times 4 = 12$ $4 \times 3 = 12$

You can divide or share the 12 eggs:

12 shared between 3 = $12 \div 3 = 4$

12 shared between 4 = $12 \div 4 = 3$

You can do multiplication in any order: $3 \times 4 = 12$ or $4 \times 3 = 12$

You have to divide the bigger number by the smaller number.

$12 \div 3 = 4$ ✓ $12 \div 4 = 3$ ✓ $4 \div 3 = 12$ ✗ $3 \div 4 = 12$ ✗

WILD FACT

KOMODO DRAGONS are the **LARGEST LIZARDS IN THE WORLD.**

Task 1

Draw arrays to find the answers to the calculations. The first one has been done for you.

3 × 2 = ⬭⬭⬭ = 6
       ⬭⬭⬭

a 2 × 4 =

b 4 × 3 =

c 6 × 2 =

Task 2

Write two multiplication facts and two division facts for each array. An example has been done for you.

4 × 2 = 8
2 × 4 = 8
8 ÷ 4 = 2
8 ÷ 2 = 4

a _____

_____

_____

_____

b _____

_____

_____

_____

Task 3

a An island has four communities of Komodo dragons. Each community has five Komodo dragons. How many dragons are on the island?

b A scientist takes three photos of Komodo dragons every day. How many photos will she have after one week?

WILD FACT

So that **PREDATORS** won't think they are a tasty snack, baby **KOMODO DRAGONS ROLL THEMSELVES IN POO!**

Now lumber to pages 114–115 to record what you have learned in your Explorer's Logbook.

Fractions

Fractions are equal parts of one whole.

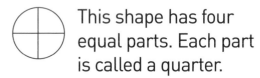 This shape has four equal parts. Each part is called a quarter.

 This shape has $\frac{1}{4}$ shaded.

 This shape has $\frac{3}{4}$ shaded.

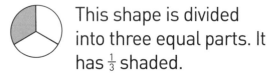 This shape is divided into three equal parts. It has $\frac{1}{3}$ shaded.

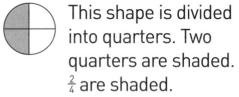 This shape is divided into quarters. Two quarters are shaded. $\frac{2}{4}$ are shaded.

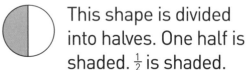 This shape is divided into halves. One half is shaded. $\frac{1}{2}$ is shaded.

You can see that $\frac{2}{4} = \frac{1}{2}$

FACT FILE

Animal:	King vulture
I live in:	The forests of Central and South America
I eat:	Dead animals

Task 1   **What fraction of each shape is shaded?**

a _____

b _____

c _____

d _____

e _____

f _____

Task 2

Shade $\frac{3}{4}$ of each of these shapes. Remember that finding a quarter is the same as halving and halving again.

 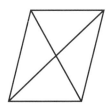 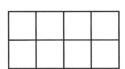  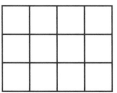

Task 3

Find the fractions of the king vulture eggs. Circle each fraction, then count the eggs in the circled fraction and write your number on the line.

a $\frac{3}{4}$ = _____ eggs

b $\frac{1}{2}$ = _____ eggs

c $\frac{1}{4}$ = _____ eggs

d $\frac{1}{3}$ = _____ eggs

Now swoop to pages 114–115 to record what you have learned in your Explorer's Logbook.

Measure

You can measure short lengths in **millimetres** (mm) and **centimetres** (cm). You can measure longer lengths in **metres** (m) and **kilometres** (km).

Look at the ruler below. You can see the cm and the mm marked on the edges.

How long is your little finger?
Measure it against the ruler.

You can measure mass in **grams** (g) and **kilograms** (kg).

You can measure capacity in **millilitres** (ml) and **litres** (l).

Look in your fridge or cupboards at home. How many millilitres or litres of liquid are in the milk carton or squash bottle? How much does a packet of biscuits or flour weigh?

You can measure temperature in **degrees** Celsius (°C).

FACT FILE

Animal: Little red flying fox
I live in: Swamps and forests of Australia
I eat: Nectar, fruit and insects

Task 1

Draw a line to match the equipment to the units each one measures. Some will have more than one unit.

grams millilitres metres kilograms degrees centimetres millimetres litres

Task 2

Circle the words to make each of these correct. An example has been done for you.

 1g   is heavier than / (is lighter than) 3g

a   250ml   holds more than / holds less than   200ml

b   14cm is longer than / is shorter than 36cm

c   36kg is heavier than / is lighter than 18kg

d   **1cm** is longer than / is shorter than **1m**

e   **1l** is less than / is more than **1ml**

f   **3kg** is heavier than / is lighter than **3g**

Task 3

Circle the most suitable measurement for each item. The first one has been done for you.

Water boils at a temperature of	10°C	(100°C)	1°C	1000°C
An apple weighs	10kg	1kg	100g	1000kg
A teaspoon holds	5ml	50l	500l	5l
The length of a pencil is	10m	1m	1mm	10cm

Now glide to pages 114–115 to record what you have learned in your Explorer's Logbook.

Money

Handwritten: 16 ✱ 20 / 32 / 5 10 / 8 3 / 16 / 3

These are the coins that you can use to pay for things:

You can also use £5, £10, £20 and £50 notes.

You might pay with coins or notes worth more than the value of what you are buying, so the shopkeeper will give back some change.

For example: If I buy an apple that costs 68p and I pay with a £1 coin, I will receive some change.

68p

£1.00 — 68p =

100 — 68 =

100 — 60 – 8 = **32p**

Task 1 — What amounts do these coins make?

a    *18p* ✓

b    *36p*

c    *57p*

FACT FILE

Animal: Jaguar
I live in: Forests, wetlands and grasslands of South and Central America
I eat: Mammals such as deer and also fish and caimans (a type of crocodile)

Task 2

Draw the coins needed to make these amounts.

a 19p

b 34p

c 88p

Task 3

a George spends 36p on a jaguar postcard. He pays with a 50p coin.

How much change will he get?

_____

b Roopa buys some sweets costing 24p.

What change will she get from £1.00?

_____

c Amy pays for a comic with this coin:

She gets these coins in change:

How much did Amy spend?

_____

WILD FACT

A **JAGUAR'S BLACK SPOTS** are called **ROSETTES,** because they are shaped like roses.

Now grab pages 114–115 to record what you have learned in your Explorer's Logbook.

Time

The **short hand** on a clock tells you what hour it is.

When the short hand is on a number and the long hand is on 12, it is 'something' o'clock.

For example:

2 o'clock   **10 o'clock**   **5 o'clock**

The **long hand** tells you how many minutes to or past the hour it is.

When the **long** hand is on **6**, it is half past the hour:	When the **long** hand is on **3**, it is quarter **past** the hour:	When the **long** hand is on **9**, it is quarter **to** the hour:

half past 2	**quarter past 8**	**quarter to 5**

When the long hand is pointing at other numbers, it shows these minutes **past** or **to** the hour:

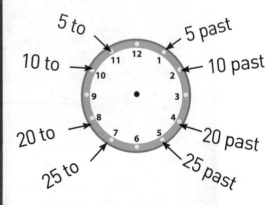

FACT FILE

Animal:	Slow loris
I live in:	Forests of south-east Asia
I eat:	Fruit, plants, nectar, insects, reptiles and eggs

Draw lines to match the times shown on the clocks to the times in the boxes.

| half past 5 | half past 10 | 8 o'clock |

Task 2

I see a slow loris eating at the following times. What times do the clocks show?

a _____ b _____ c _____

_____ _____ _____

Task 3

A scientist is studying slow lorises in the wild. At what times did he spot the animals?

a _____ b _____ c _____ d _____

_____ _____ _____ _____

WILD FACT

SLOW LORISES often **EAT** hanging **UPSIDE DOWN** from branches with their **FEET**.

Now creep to pages 114–115 to record what you have learned in your Explorer's Logbook.

2D shapes

Two-dimensional (2D) shapes are flat:

circle triangle square rectangle pentagon hexagon octagon

Two sides meet at a corner.
A circle has no sides, just a curve.

The shapes above all fold exactly in half.
The fold is a **line of symmetry**.

Folding on the line of symmetry:

WILD FACT

RHINOCEROS BEETLES are really strong. Male beetles can LIFT up to 100 TIMES their own BODYWEIGHT!

Task 1	How many sides does each shape have?

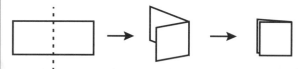

a ___ b ___ c ___ d ___ e ___ f ___ g ___

Task 2 Without looking at the facing page, draw lines to match these shapes to their names.

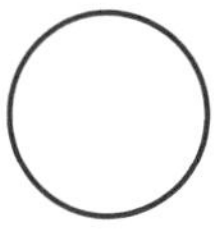

square

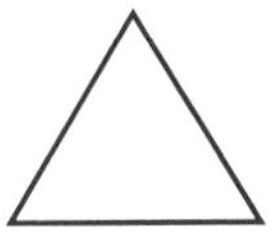

rectangle

circle

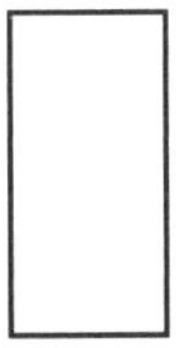

triangle

WILD FACT

MALE RHINOCEROS BEETLES use their HORNS to FIGHT EACH OTHER.

Task 3 Complete the symmetrical patterns on each shape. The first one has been done for you.

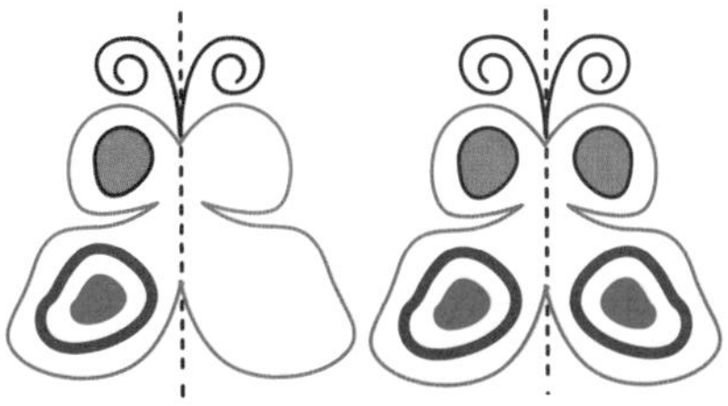

a 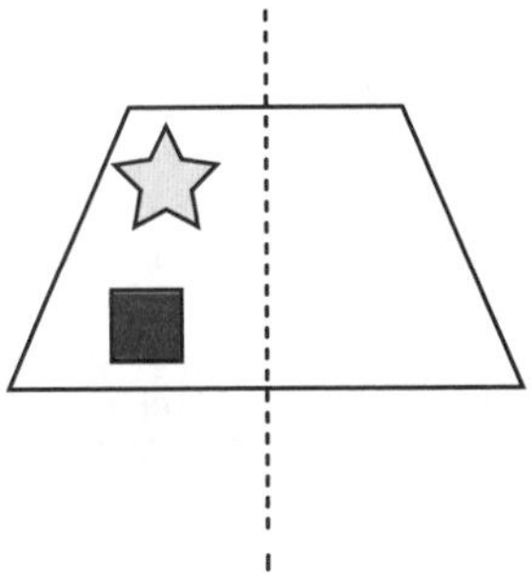   b 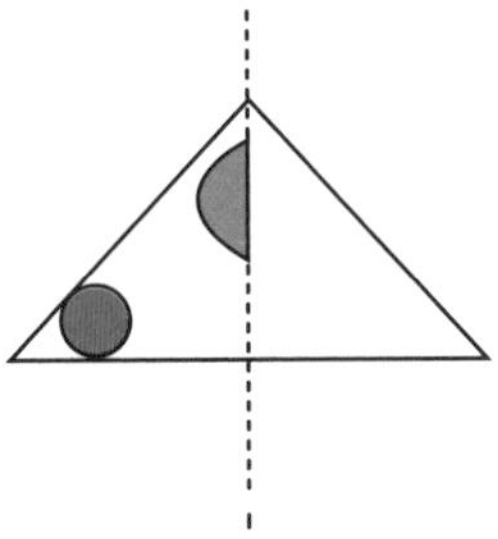   c 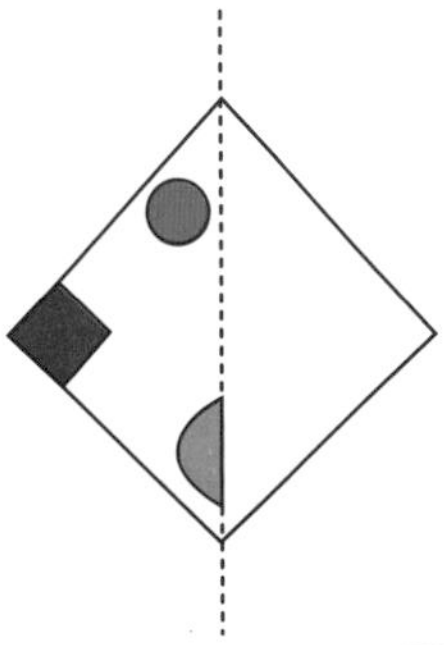   d

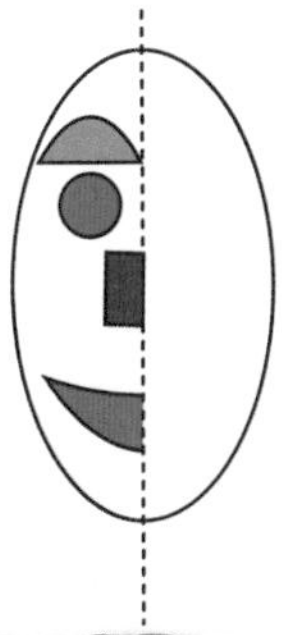

Now scuttle to pages 114–115 to record what you have learned in your Explorer's Logbook.

3D shapes

Three-dimensional (3D) shapes are solid shapes that can be picked up.

3D shapes have faces, edges and vertices (corners). One corner is called a vertex.

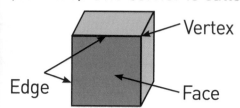

Vertex

Edge

Face

Here are some 3D shapes:

 sphere

 cube

cuboid

cylinder

square pyramid

tetrahedron

triangular prism

 cone

You can see 3D shapes in everyday life:

Task 1

This shape is called a _____.

How many vertices, faces and edges does this shape have?

Vertices _____   Faces _____   Edges _____

Task 2 Write the shapes in the correct boxes below. One has been done for you.

cube

cuboid

cylinder

square pyramid

triangular prism

tetrahedron

cone

Shapes with only straight edges	Shapes with curved edges
cube	

WILD FACT

KINKAJOUS use their **LONG TAILS** for balance and to **HANG FROM TREES.** They can even use their tails as a **BLANKET** to keep **WARM!**

Task 3 The faces of each 3D shape are 2D shapes. What 2D shapes make up these 3D shapes? An example has been done for you.

is made up of 4 triangles and 1 square.

 a is made up of _____ .

 b is made up of _____ and

_____ .

 c is made up of _____ and

_____ .

Now head over to pages 114–115 to record what you have learned in your Explorer's Logbook.

Statistics

You can use charts and tables to show information. The information on these charts and tables can be used to answer questions.

You can use digits (1, 2, 3 ...) or tallies to record things you count.

For example:

1	2	3	4	5

Then you can count the total in fives and ones.

= 5 + 5 + 2

Task 1

Four children counted the number of katydids in a woodland. Here are their results on a tally chart.

	Number of katydids	Total
Adam		9
Zeikel		
Joel		
Meera		

a The table shows that Adam spotted 9 katydids. Write the totals for the other three children.

b Who spotted the most katydids? _____

c Who spotted the fewest? _____

Task 2 A group of scientists measured the amount of rain that fell in a rainforest. This block diagram shows their results.

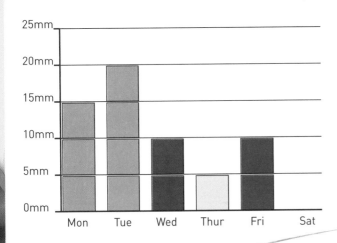

a On which day did least rain fall?

_____

b How much rain fell on Monday?

_____

c On which two days did the same amount of rain fall?

_____

_____

d 25 mm of rain fell on Saturday. Add this information to the block diagram.

Task 3 A scientist is counting katydids. She counts how many she can see in the trees, on the grass, on leaves and on logs. She shows her results as a pictogram:

 = 2 katydids

Trees

Grass

Leaves

Logs

a How many katydids were found in each area?

Trees: _____   **Grass:** _____

Leaves: _____   **Logs:** _____

b How many katydids were found altogether?

_____

WILD FACT

KATYDIDS' **EARS** are on their **FRONT LEGS!**

Now hop to pages 114–115 to record what you have learned in your Explorer's Logbook.

Quick quiz

Now try these questions. Give yourself 1 mark for every correct answer.

```
0  1  2  3  4  5  6  7  8  9  10 11 12 13 14 15 16 17 18 19 20 21 22 23 24 25 26 27 28 29 30
```

1 **What are the next three numbers? Use the number line above to help you.**

    a   2   4   6   8   ____   ____   ____

    b   4   7   10   ____   ____   ____

    c   25   20   15   ____   ____   ____

2 **Put these six numbers in order from smallest to largest.**

    12   27   3   46   84   58

    smallest _____ largest

3 **Use the number line at the top of the page to help you answer these.**

    a $13 + 5 =$ _____   **b** $26 - 4 =$ _____

4 **Work out the answers to these.**

    a $18 + 20 =$ _____   **b** $55 - 30 =$ _____

5 **Find some counters or buttons to help you to answer these.**

    a $7 \times 2 =$ _____   **b** $15 \div 3 =$ _____

6 **Draw a circle around the sets that have $\frac{3}{4}$ shaded.**

   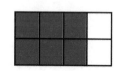

7 **Shade $\frac{1}{4}$ of the group of ladybirds.**

8 Measure the length of the worm below.

_____

9 Write the units in the box below under the correct heading.
One has been done for you.

centimetres   grams   kilometres   millilitres
millimetres   kilograms   litres   metres

Length	Mass	Capacity
centimetres		

10 How much money will you have if you have all these coins?

_____

11 What time does each clock show?

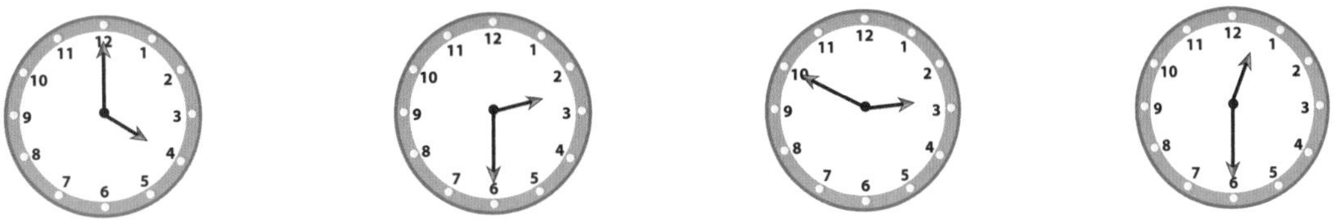

a _____   b _____   c _____   d _____

12 Match each shape to its name.

rectangle   sphere   triangle   cylinder   cube   cuboid   square pyramid

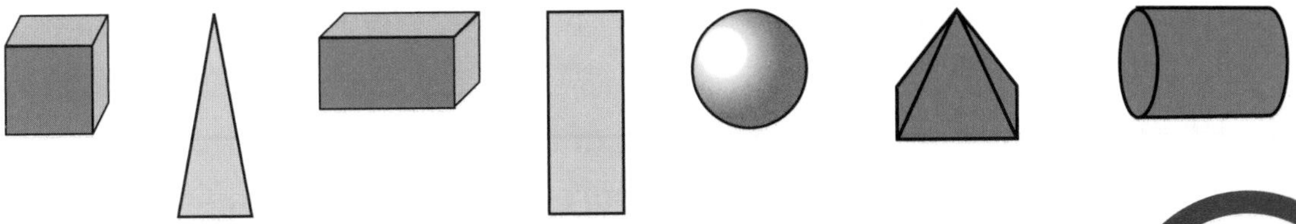

How did you do?   1–5 Try again!   6–10 Good try!
11–15 Great work!   16–20 Excellent exploring!

/20

Consonants and vowels

Words are made up of letters called **consonants** and **vowels**.

Most of the letters in the alphabet are consonants:

b, c, d, f, g, h, j, k, l, m, n, p, q, r, s, t, v, w, x, y, z

When two consonants come together, they make a **digraph** if they make a single sound.

For example:

ch *chop*   **sh** *shoe*   **ll** *sill*

If two consonants come together and each consonant makes its own sound, they make a **consonant blend**.

For example:

st *list*   **fl** *flop*   **gr** *grip*

There are five vowels: **a, e, i, o, u**

Most words have at least one vowel. Some words begin with a vowel: *elephant* begins with a vowel.

Some words have more than one vowel.
For example, there are three vowels in *elephant*:
e, e, a

FACT FILE

Animal:	Asian elephant
I live in:	Grasslands and forests of Asia
I eat:	Roots, grasses, leaves, bark and fruits
I weigh:	About 5000 kg

Task 1   Write one vowel in the gap in each of these simple words. Then read the word. Some have more than one possible answer.

a f__x   **c** k__d   **e** c__n   **g** y__s   **i** w__t

b t__b   **d** l__d   **f** r__g   **h** j__m   **j** z__p

Task 2

Put a vowel into each gap to make a word with a consonant blend or a digraph at the beginning.

a ch___p

b fl___t

c sp___n

d gr___b

e sw___m

f tr___p

g dr___g

h sh___d

i pl___n

j th___t

k sl___t

l tr___m

Task 3

Put a vowel into each gap to make a word with a consonant blend or a digraph at the end.

a l___ts

b m___ch

c s___ng

d n___ck

e b___nd

f c___mp

g w___nt

h v___st

i g____ft

j b___lb

k l___nk

l k___pt

Task 4

Add vowels into these longer words. They are in sentences to help you.

a The **d___nt___st** looks after your teeth.

b The **r___ck___t** went up to the moon.

c A **r___b___n** is a bird that lives in the garden.

d At Halloween we use a **p___mpk___n** to make a lantern.

Now lumber to pages 116–117 to record what you have learned in your Explorer's Logbook.

Phonics and decodable words

Words are made up of consonants, vowels, digraphs and trigraphs put together.

Trigraphs are when three letters are put together to make one sound, for example, **tch** as in *stitch* and **dge** as in *hedge*.

Here are some of the words from the Wild Facts about the silkworm. They all have a consonant blend.

stop	*just*	*spin*	*silk*

You can split words to make them easier to read:

st-op	ju-st	sp-in	si-lk

Task 1   Draw lines to join word beginnings with word endings to make whole words.

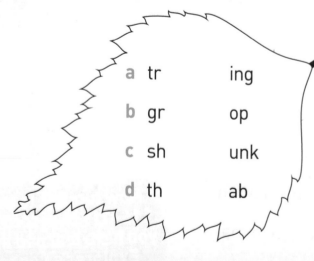

a	tr		ing
b	gr		op
c	sh		unk
d	th		ab

WILD FACT

The **SILKWORM** is a caterpillar. As soon as it hatches, it **EATS MULBERRY LEAVES** non-stop for **35 DAYS!**

FACT FILE

Animal:	Silkworm
I live in:	Mulberry trees around the world
I eat:	Mulberry leaves
I weigh:	About 3.5 g

Task 2   Some of these words are made up and do not make sense! Circle the real words.

a   take   jom   flop   bake   shiz

b   blemp   jam   pline   week   twin

c   soggy   dack   flow   teeb   hoob

d   doy   chop   kill   silk   jall

WILD FACT

The SILKWORM spins 300–900 METRES of SILK FIBRE in just 3 days to make a COCOON around itself. The silk can be used to make clothes.

Task 3   Make up your own nonsense words by using the beginning of one real word and the ending of another.

a   _____

b   _____

c   _____

Task 4   The table shows words with consonant blends, digraphs and trigraphs. Put a tick in one box for each row to show which each word has. The first one has been done for you.

	Consonant blend	Digraph	Trigraph
such		✓	
catch			
stay			
hedge			
shut			
duck			

Now wriggle to pages 116–117 to record what you have learned in your Explorer's Logbook.

Double letters at the end of words

When the sounds **f**, **s**, **z** and **l** are at the end of a word, they are often doubled: **ff**, **ss**, **zz**, **ll**, for example, in the words *stiff*, *cross*, *fizz* and *ball*.

Some words have **c** and **k** at the end. Together they make the sound **k**.
For example, *trick*.

Task 1

Explore the Wild Facts and find two words that end with 'ck'. Write them on the lines.

_____

_____

Task 2

Add **ck** to each of these words and read them.

a thi____

b bla____

c so____

d pe____

e sho____

f fli____

g mu____

h qua____

WILD FACT

The **MALE PEAFOWL** is called a **PEACOCK.** It has bright blue and green feathers. The **FEMALE PEAHEN** is **DULL BROWN, WHITE AND BLACK,** with some green and blue on the neck.

Task 3

Choose one of the digraphs from the box to complete each of these words. Some of them have more than one answer.

ff	ss	ll	zz

a ja_____

b dre_____

c pu_____

d me_____

e bu_____

f cli_____

g che_____

h mi_____

Task 4

Some words in these sentences are incomplete. Add a vowel and one of the double letters to complete the words. Use the pictures to help you.

ff	ss	ll	zz	ck

a I found a sh ___ ___ ___ on the beach.

b I love to k___ ___ ___ a b___ ___ ___.

c My hat blew ___ ___ ___ in the wind.

d I like to hear the bees b ___ ___ ___.

e My brother made such a f___ ___ ___ when he f___ ___ ___ down.

WILD FACT

A BABY PEAFOWL is called a PEACHICK.

Now strut to pages 116–117 to record what you have learned in your Explorer's Logbook.

Word endings ve and y

Sometimes words end in unexpected ways.

Orangutans live in trees.

There is a **v** sound at the end of *live* as the **e** is silent.

There are different ways of pronouncing a **y** when it comes at the end of a word. It can sound like **ee** as in *happy*, but it can also sound like **eye** as in *fly*.

WILD FACT

The **ORANGUTAN** is the **HEAVIEST** animal to live in a **TREE.**

Task 1   Choose one of the words from the box to fill each of the gaps.

have	twelve	love	sleeve	shave	wave

a My dad has a __ __ __ __ __ every day.

b I __ __ __ __ __ watching the orangutans play.

c When I go home, I __ __ __ __ __ goodbye to my friends.

d My arm slides into my __ __ __ __ __ __ __.

e There are __ __ __ __ __ __ __ eggs in the box.

f I __ __ __ __ __ a drink of milk before I go to bed.

FACT FILE

Animal: Orangutan
I live in: Trees in the forests of south-east Asia
I eat: Fruit, plants and insects
I weigh: 35 to 100 kg

Task 2

Write two words that rhyme with the word at the beginning of each line.

a **save** _____ _____

b **five** _____ _____

c **love** _____ _____

d **give** _____ _____

e **leave** _____ _____

WILD FACT

The **ORANGUTAN'S ARMSPAN** (from fingertip to fingertip) is **LONGER** than its whole **BODY!**

Task 3

Read the words in the box then put them into the correct group. The first two have been done for you.

| ~~try~~ ~~very~~ fly spy merry fairy cry fry happy why |
| shy puppy silly candy my windy mummy by |

Words with a 'y' ending that sounds like 'eye'	Words with a 'y' ending that sounds like 'ee'
try	very

Now swing to pages 116–117 to record what you have learned in your Explorer's Logbook.

Adding s or es to nouns and verbs

A noun is a person, place, or thing. To make many nouns plural (more than one person, place or thing), you can just add **s**, but some nouns ending with certain letters need **es**.

Nouns ending in **a**, **b**, **d**, **e**, **f**, **ff**, **g**, **gg**, **ck**, **l**, **ll**, **m**, **n**, **p**, **r**, **t**, **w**: make these plural by adding **s**.

For example: *bats*, *chicks*, *eggs*

Nouns ending in **s**, **ss**, **x**, **zz**, **ch**, **tch**, **sh**: make these plural by adding **es**.

For example: *boxes*, *stitches*, *buses*

Sometimes a verb (a doing or being word) needs to be changed in the same way.

WILD FACT

The **LARGEST** bats in the world are species of **FRUIT BAT.**

Task 1   Make these singular nouns into plurals by adding **s** or **es**.

a cat___   witch___   banana___   fox___   brush___

b dog___   window___   church___   chip___   kiss___

c bus___   toy___   lad___   cliff___   dish___

d animal___   duck___   pill___   cow___   class___

Task 2

Circle the correct plural for each of these nouns.

a **glass**   glasss   glasses   g **apple**   applees   apples

b **broom**   brooms   broomes   h **bush**   bushs   bushes

c **watch**   watches   watchs   i **peg**   pegs   peges

d **six**   sixs   sixes   j **truck**   trucks   truckes

e **lunch**   lunches   lunchs

f **dolphin**   dolphins   dolphines

WILD FACT

The **FRUIT BAT** (also known as the **FLYING FOX**) can smell **RIPE FRUIT** that is as far as **5 KM (3 MILES)** away.

FACT FILE

Animal: Fruit bat
I live in: Dense forests of southern Asia
I eat: Fruit juices and flower nectar
I weigh: Up to 1.5 kg

Task 3

Fill in the missing words by adding **s** or **es** to the bold verbs in these sentences.

a I **run** to see the fruit bat.

Millie _____ to see the fruit bat.

b I **show** my picture to my mum.

Sam _____ his picture to his mum.

c I **hiss** loudly. The snake _____ loudly.

d I **ring** the doorbell. Fred _____ the doorbell.

e I **fix** the lock on the box. Dad _____ the lock on the box.

f I **fill** my glass with water. Mum _____ my glass with water.

Now fly to pages 116–117 to record what you have learned in your Explorer's Logbook.

Adding ing or ed to verbs

Verbs are **doing** or **being** words. Sometimes you can use the simple form of the word. This is called the **root word**.

For example:

sting   *lift*   *push*   *talk*

You can add **ing** or **ed** at the end of the word to change the way it is used, without needing to change the spelling of the word itself.

For example:

sting ⟶ *stinging*   *lift* ⟶ *lifted*

FACT FILE

Animal:	Scorpion
I live in:	Various types of habitat including deserts, rainforests, grasslands and the seashore
I eat:	Insects and small animals
I weigh:	Up to 50 g

Task 1   Add **ing** and **ed** to each of these root words. The first one has been done for you.

climb   climbing   climbed

a **inject**   _____ _____

b **stay**   _____ _____

c **weigh**   _____ _____

Task 2

These verbs describe what a scorpion does. Add **ing** and **ed** to each of them.

a hunt _____ _____

b pinch _____ _____

c crawl _____ _____

Task 3

Make your own list of verbs that can be changed in the same way without altering the root word.

_____

_____

Task 4

These words all end with **ng**. Add **ng** to each word and read the word.

a sa____ ____

b thi____ ____

c go____ ____

d bri____ ____

e hu____ ____

f belo____ ____

g ri____ ____

h lu____ ____

i ki____ ____

j fa____ ____

k ru____ ____

l po____ ____

Now scurry to pages 116–117 to record what you have learned in your Explorer's Logbook.

71

Using double vowel digraphs

You already know that a digraph is a single sound made with two letters. The sound it makes is called a **phoneme**. A **grapheme** is the written form of that sound, for example, consonant digraphs like **ch**, **sh**, **ck**.

Sometimes, double vowels in words create a phoneme. For example, you can double **o** to make **oo**, as in *fool*. Make a circle with your lips and say that sound.

You can also use double **e** to make **ee**, as in *feet*. Now widen your mouth and say that sound.

FACT FILE

Animal:	Red panda
I live in:	The cold mountain forests of Asia
I eat:	Bamboo, fruit, flowers and eggs
I weigh:	3 to 6 kg

Task 1 **Read this passage about the red panda. Find and write four words with the oo grapheme.**

The red panda is much smaller than the giant panda. It has red and white markings on its face, and a striped tail like a raccoon. You might see it eating food such as bamboo shoots and leaves.

_____   _____

_____   _____

Task 2 Complete these **oo** words. Make the second word rhyme with the first word.

a m__ __n   s__ __ __

b h__ __p   l__ __ __

c z__ __m   b__ __ __

d f__ __d   m__ __ __ __

Task 3 Now hunt about in the Wild Facts to find two words with the **ee** grapheme. Write them on the lines.

_____

_____

Task 4 Find more words with **ee** that rhyme with these words. The first letter is given each time to help you.

a seek   w__ __ __

b peep   k__ __ __

c sheet   m__ __ __ __

d need   w__ __ __

e feel   h__ __ __ __

Now scamper to pages 116–117 to record what you have learned in your Explorer's Logbook.

The graphemes ie, i-e, igh, y, oy and oi

Many words have graphemes that sound the same but are made up of different digraphs and trigraphs.

These digraphs and trigraphs sound the same: **ie**, **i-e**, **igh**, **y**.

In the same way, **oi** and **oy** sound the same. The **oy** digraph usually comes at the end of a word, for example, *boy*.

The digraph **oi** is usually in the middle of a word, for example, *noise*.

Task 1

Write two words that rhyme with each of these.

a **boy** _____ _____

b **coil** _____ _____

c **groin** _____ _____

Task 2 Write a word spelled with **oi** or **oy** in these sentences.

a I have a sore throat and I have lost my v__ __ __ __.

b I like to j__ __ __ in with all the games.

c I planted a seed in the s__ __ __.

d The referee tossed a c__ __ __ to see who would start.

e I found my car in the t__ __ box.

f Stop cheating! You will s__ __ __ __ the game!

WILD FACT

The **SALTWATER CROCODILE** is the **LARGEST** of all the **REPTILES.** It can grow to **6 M LONG.**

WILD FACT

SALTWATER CROCODILES hide in murky water and mud. They **LIE IN WAIT** for their prey and then **LUNGE FORWARD** and snap their **POWERFUL JAWS** together!

Task 3 Use the words in the box to complete the sentences. The first letter of each word has been given to help you.

light	tight	lie	tie	side	bite
like	kite	cry	fly	my	

a It was dark, so I put on the l__ __ __ __.

b When I l__ __ in bed, I turn on my s__ __ __ __.

c I b__ __ __ on my apple.

d My brother upset me and made me c__ __.

e I t__ __ the string in a t__ __ __ __ __ knot.

f I l__ __ __ __ to f__ __ m__ k__ __ __.

Now lunge forward to pages 116–117 to record what you have learned in your Explorer's Logbook.

The phoneme s

When a letter **c** is followed by a letter **e**, letter **i** or letter **y**, it makes an **s** sound.

For example:

ce → *ice*

ci → *pencil*

cy → *fancy*

FACT FILE

Animal: Asiatic black bear
I live in: Forests, hills and mountains
I eat: Leaves, nuts, fruits, berries, eggs, insects, birds and small mammals
I weigh: 60 to 220 kg

WILD FACT

ASIATIC BLACK BEARS' **CLAWS** are **STRONG** and this makes them excellent **CLIMBERS.**

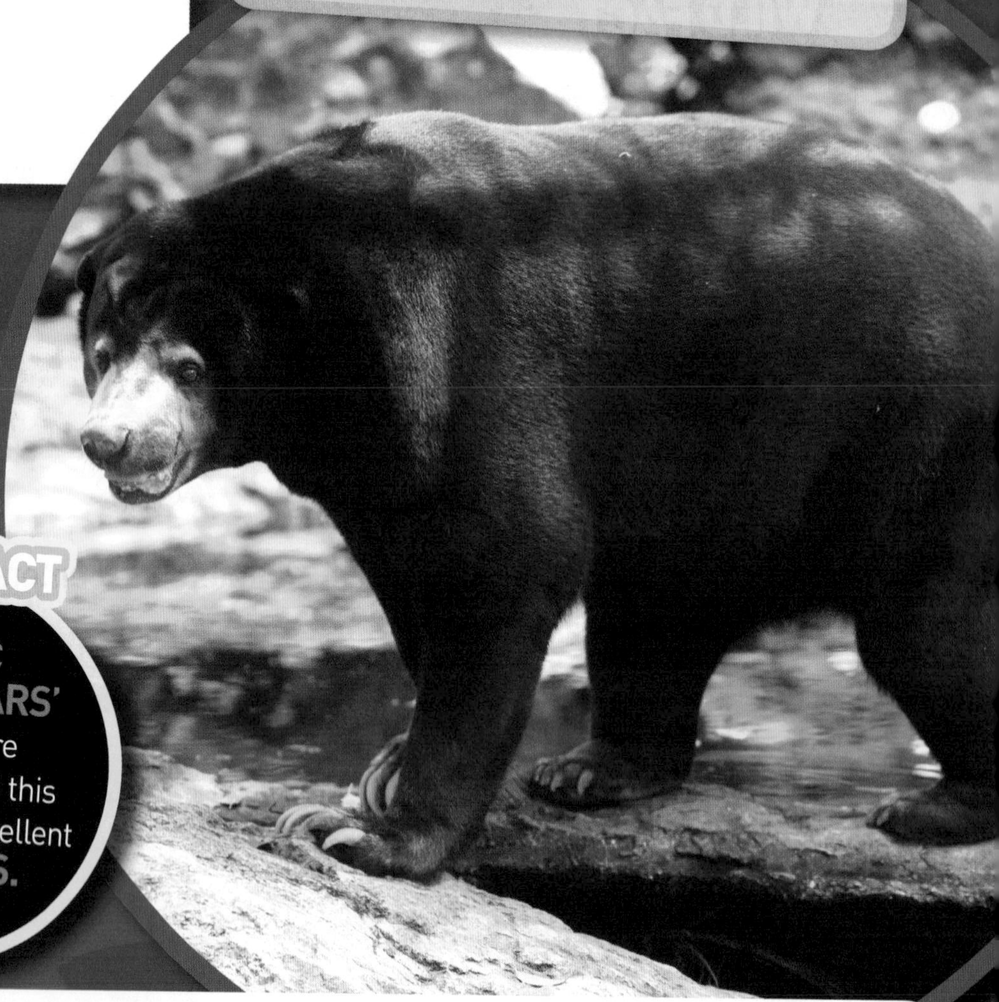

Task 1 Write three words that rhyme with **ace** and **ice**.

a **ace** ____________ ____________ ____________

b **ice** ____________ ____________ ____________

Task 2   Underline all the words in the bear where the **c** is sounded **s**.

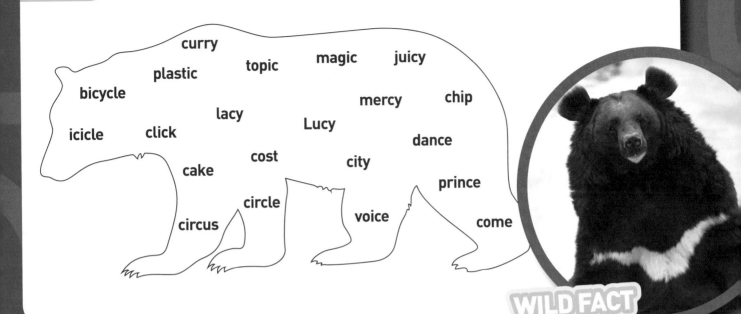

curry

topic   magic   juicy

plastic

bicycle   mercy   chip

lacy

icicle   click   Lucy

dance

cost   city

cake

prince

circle

voice   come

circus

WILD FACT

The **ASIATIC BLACK BEAR** has a **CREAM, CRESCENT-SHAPED** marking on its **CHEST**, so it is often called the **MOON BEAR.**

Task 3   Fill in the crossword with words spelled with a **c** followed by **e**, **i** or **y**.

Across

2 You run to win this.

4 A rocket shoots up into this.

5 I f _ _ _ _ an ice cream.

Down

1 The country on the other side of the English Channel.

3 Sugar and s _ _ _ _ and all things nice.

		¹F		
	²R			
³S	■			
⁴S				
	■			
⁵F				

Now clamber to pages 116–117 to record what you have learned in your Explorer's Logbook.

Silent letters

Lots of words have **silent letters**.
A silent letter is a letter that cannot be heard when the word is spoken.

Here are some examples of silent letters:

c after **s**   ⟶   *scene*

k before **n**   ⟶   *knight*

w before **r**   ⟶   *wrap*

b after **m**   ⟶   *crumb*

h after **g**   ⟶   *ghost*

Sometimes other letters are silent in a word, for example: **l, u, t, n, s**.

WILD FACT

The **TIGER** is the **BIGGEST WILD CAT** in the **WORLD.**

Task 1   **Read these sentences then search for the words that have silent letters. Underline them.**

a My knees began to knock when I saw the tiger.

b Jack said he had seen a ghost.

c I know that Tom got it wrong.

d Asif tried to guess the song I played on the guitar.

e Daisy cut her thumb while knitting.

f Rowan fell down and broke his wrist.

FACT FILE

Animal: Bengal tiger
I live in: Swamps, grasslands and rainforests
I eat: Wild boar, deer and many other animals
I weigh: Up to 300 kg

Task 2   Find and circle two words in each line which have a silent letter.

a game   gnome   groan   wrap

b plum   doubt   numb   tent

c column   king   wring   kind

d gnat   grain   guide   stick

e wriggle   smart   hatch   crumb

WILD FACT

TIGERS live in areas full of trees, bushes and clumps of tall grass, where **THEIR STRIPES CAMOUFLAGE** them.

Task 3   Spot the word that has the silent letter and underline it.

a **silent c:**   scorch   scamp   scissors   scar

b **silent l:**   tail   talk   look   wild

c **silent s:**   island   inside   igloos   illness

d **silent t:**   bitter   filter   listen   wilted

e **silent n:**   auntie   name   under   autumn

Now prowl to pages 116–117 to record what you have learned in your Explorer's Logbook.

er and est

You can describe animals and objects by using **adjectives**.

Then you can add **er** to the adjective to show it is **more than** as you described.

You can add **est** to the adjective to show that it is **the most** it could be.

For example:

A <u>long</u> snake

A <u>longer</u> snake

The <u>longest</u> snake

If there is already an **e** at the end of the word, you just need to add **r** or **st**.

FACT FILE

Animal:	Burmese python
I live in:	Jungles and marshes in south-east Asia
I eat:	Animals and birds
I weigh:	About 35 kg

WILD FACT

BURMESE PYTHONS are usually about 3.5 M LONG but they have been known to GROW to 5.7 M!

Task 1

Add **er** and **est** to each of these adjectives and then read them. The first one has been done for you.

hard	harder	hardest
a **cool**	_____	_____
b **soft**	_____	_____
c **great**	_____	_____

Task 2 Add **r** and **st** to each of these adjectives and then read them. The first one has been done for you.

late   later   latest

a wise   _____   _____

b simple   _____   _____

c strange   _____   _____

Task 3 When words have just one vowel in the middle and one consonant at the end, that last consonant is doubled. Double the last consonant, then add **er** and **est** to each of these adjectives and then read them. The first one has been done for you.

fit   fitter   fittest

a red   _____   _____

b sad   _____   _____

c hot   _____   _____

Task 4 When words end in **y**, we change the **y** to an **i** before adding **er** or **est**. Change the **y** to an **i**, then add **er** and **est** to each of these adjectives. Now read them. The first one has been done for you.

busy   busier   busiest

a silly   _____   _____

b lazy   _____   _____

c funny   _____   _____

Now slither to pages 116–117 to record what you have learned in your Explorer's Logbook.

Homophones

Homophones are two or more words that sound the same but have different meanings and spellings.

Search the Wild Facts and find a word that sounds like *there* (meaning 'in that place'). Yes, you're right... it is *their* (meaning 'belonging to them').

FACT FILE

Animal:	Bactrian camel
I live in:	Deserts and grasslands in Central Asia
I eat:	Grass, plants, leaves and seeds
I weigh:	300 to 650 kg

Task 1 Read the sentences below and fill in the gaps by using **there** or **their** in the right places.

a The children took ___ ___ ___ ___ ___ dog for a walk.

b Look at that camel over ___ ___ ___ ___ ___!

c ___ ___ ___ ___ ___ are lots of camels in Asia.

d The dogs wagged ___ ___ ___ ___ ___ tails when they saw ___ ___ ___ ___ ___ owner.

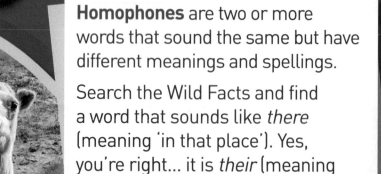

WILD FACT

If **CAMELS FEEL THREATENED,** they will **SPIT.** Their **CHEEKS BULGE** just before they are about to spit. So stand well back!

Task 2   Choose the correct homophone from the brackets to complete the sentence.

a   I went to the shops to _____ an apple.   **(buy / by)**

b   I have been waiting all _____ to see a camel.   **(week / weak)**

c   The wind _____ the sand across the desert.   **(blue / blew)**

WILD FACT

Wild **BACTRIAN CAMELS** can drink **WATER** that is **SALTIER** than the sea!

Task 3   Choose the homophone from the box that makes sense to complete the sentences.

to	too	two

a   It was much _____ hot in the desert.

b   We went _____ see the camels in the zoo.

c   Bactrian camels have _____ humps each.

Now step to pages 116–117 to record what you have learned in your Explorer's Logbook.

Quick quiz

Now try these questions. Give yourself 1 mark for every correct answer.

1 Add the correct endings to these adjectives so that they show **more than** and **the most** for each one.

/4

  a smart _____   _____

  b easy   _____   _____

  c wet   _____   _____

  d nice   _____   _____

2 Change these singular nouns into plural nouns by adding **s** or **es** at the end.

/3

  a brush_____   **b** cub_____   **c** cave_____

3 Write the homophone that makes sense in each sentence.

/6

  deer / dear

  a There are many _____ roaming in the woods.

  b You are my _____ friend.

  not / knot

  c I have a _____ in my shoe lace.

  d A camel's spit is _____ very pleasant!

  write / right

  e I will _____ a letter to my grandma.

  f I am _____-handed, but my mum is left-handed.

4 Put a vowel into each space in the words so that the sentences make sense.

/4

  a I adopted a r__bb__t that needed a n__w h__me.

  b My d__d w__nt to the sh__ps.

  c The c__p of m__lk was very h__t.

  d I love f__sh and ch__ps for my d__nn__r.

5 Make **five** words out of these consonants, vowels and trigraphs.

/1

Consonants	Vowels	Trigraphs
c w h d b	a e i o u	tch dge

_____   _____   _____

_____   _____

6 Write a rhyming word for each word. They must all have a silent letter.

a crumb _____   **b** life _____

c long _____   **d** toast _____

e fist _____

7 Write **five** words where the letter **c** makes an **s** sound.

_____   _____   _____

_____   _____

8 Complete these words using **ck**, **ff**, **ll**, **ss** or **zz**.

a bri__ __   **b** acro__ __   **c** flu__ __

d tri__ __   **e** whi__ __   **f** dre__ __

g hu__ __   **h** sti__ __   **i** ta__ __

9 Write a rhyming word that is also spelled with **oo** for each of these words.

a roof _____   **b** pool _____

c hoot _____

10 Complete these words using **ie**, **i-e**, **igh** or **y**.

Some have more than one answer.

a b_____   **b** h_____   **c** l_____

d fl_____   **e** tr_____   **f** sh_____

11 Add **ed** or **ing** to complete the words so that the sentences make sense.

a I was go_____ to school when I met a dog.

b The lady show_____ me the way to the park.

c I have always want_____ a hamster.

d The fruit bat is fly_____ in and out of the trees.

e The scorpion dart_____ towards the rocks.

f The python is slither_____ away.

12 Add a word ending in **y** that rhymes with the last word of the first line.

a I wish I could fly,

High, high in the _____.

b The day was warm and sunny,

The clown was very _____.

Capital letters

You should use **capital letters** at the start of sentences, and for the names of people, places, days and months. You should also use a capital letter to write the word 'I'.

For example:

> capital letter for person's name
>
> *My mum, Chloe and I went shopping to get new shoes.*
>
> capital letter at start of sentence   capital letter for word 'I'

> capital letter for month of the year
>
> *On Tuesday 8th September, we are going to London.*
>
> capital letter for day of the week   capital letter for name of a place

Task 1 Decide why the underlined words in each sentence start with a capital letter. Put a tick in the correct column.

	Person's name	Place name	Day of the week	Month of the year
Last <u>Saturday</u>, I went to the aquarium in <u>Manchester</u>.				
Next <u>August</u>, we are going to <u>North America</u>.				
<u>Jack</u> saw a film about crabs in <u>London</u>.				

Task 2

What is wrong with each word in red in these sentences? Write the words correctly on the lines.

a   Erin and **i** hope that we will see horseshoe crabs when we go on holiday in **july**.

_____   _____

b   We are going to the world's largest aquarium in **atlanta**, which is a city in the **united states**.

_____   _____

WILD FACT

The **HORSESHOE CRAB** uses its **TAIL** to steer through the water or to **FLIP ITSELF OVER** if it gets **STUCK** upside down.

Task 3

Circle the words in the passage below that should start with a capital letter. The first one has been done for you. Write the correct version on the lines below.

(last) friday, rosewood primary went to blue planet aquarium in chester. we saw all sorts of underwater creatures. mrs smith said that we would be starting a project on sea life. my friend marcus and i took lots of photographs, which his dad, mr jones, is going to print out.

Last _____

_____

_____

_____

_____

Steer yourself to pages 118–119 to record what you have learned in your Explorer's Logbook.

Statements and questions

A sentence must start with a **capital letter** and end with a **full stop**, a **question mark** or an **exclamation mark**. There are different types of sentence.

A **statement** is a sentence that tells you something. It starts with a capital letter and ends with a full stop.

A shark has hundreds of teeth.

A **question** is a sentence that asks something. It starts with a capital letter and ends with a question mark.

What do sharks eat?

Task 1 Rewrite each sentence, using the correct punctuation.

a a shark can grow to be as big as a bus

_____

_____

b do all sharks eat meat

_____

c there are about 460 species of shark

_____

d have you seen my book about sharks

_____

WILD FACT

GREAT WHITE SHARKS can **SMELL BLOOD** in water up to **5 KM** **(3 MILES)** away.

FACT FILE

Animal:	Great white shark
I live in:	Cool coastal waters
I eat:	Sea lions, seals and dolphins
I weigh:	Up to 2250 kg

Task 2 Decide whether each sentence is a statement or a question. Put a tick in the correct column.

Sentence	Statement	Question
Are there any sharks in Great Britain?		
Sharks have rows and rows of teeth.		
Which species of shark is the biggest?		
Great white sharks can move at speeds of up to 24 km/h (15 mph).		

WILD FACT

GREAT WHITE SHARKS have about **300 SHARP TEETH.** They don't use them to **CHEW THEIR FOOD** – they tear off big chunks of meat and swallow them whole.

Task 3 What three questions would you ask a shark expert?

Write your questions on the line. Remember to punctuate each one correctly.

a _____

_____

b _____

_____

c _____

_____

Now slice through the water to pages 118–119 to record what you have learned in your Explorer's Logbook.

Exclamations and commands

An **exclamation** is a sentence that shows a strong feeling, like anger, pain, delight or surprise. It starts with a capital letter and ends with an exclamation mark.

There's a huge shark following our boat!

A **command** is a sentence that tells you to do something. It starts with a capital letter and ends with either a full stop or an exclamation mark.

Look at that puffer fish.

The word *look* is a command verb. It is telling you what to do.

WILD FACT

One **PUFFER FISH** has **ENOUGH VENOM** to KILL 30 ADULT HUMANS!

Task 1   Punctuate each sentence correctly.
Write each sentence as an exclamation on the line.

a   what an enormous puffer fish

_____

b   look at that amazing coral

_____

c   i can't believe how big that puffer fish can puff itself up

_____

_____

Task 2   Underline the command verb in each sentence.

a Watch the puffer fish carefully.

b Take a photograph of it swimming.

c Stick the photograph in your book.

d Write a sentence about it.

FACT FILE

Animal: Puffer fish
I live in: Warm water of the Indian Ocean, Atlantic Ocean and Pacific Ocean
I eat: Mussels, clams and worms
I weigh: Up to 13 kg

Task 3   Imagine that you are telling a puffer fish what to do.

Write three commands that you would give it. An example has been done for you.

Show me how you puff yourself up. _____

a _____

b _____

c _____

Now puff yourself up and swim to pages 118–119 to record what you have learned in your Explorer's Logbook.

And, or, but

You can make one longer sentence from two shorter ones by joining words and clauses with **and**, **or** and **but**. The sentence must still make sense.

For example: *Ollie likes football. Ollie likes rugby.* These two sentences can be joined like this: *Ollie likes football and rugby.*

You can join: *Stella plays netball. She doesn't play tennis.*

Like this: *Stella plays netball but she doesn't play tennis.*

And: *Millie doesn't like peas. Millie doesn't like carrots.*

Can be written as: *Millie doesn't like peas or carrots.*

FACT FILE

Animal:	Common octopus
I live in:	Shallow, warm tropical water and temperate water, including southern coasts of the UK
I eat:	Clams, shrimps, lobsters and crabs
I weigh:	Up to 10 kg

WILD FACT

An **OCTOPUS** can **CHANGE** the **COLOUR** of **ITS SKIN** to match its surroundings and hide from danger.

Task 1   **Write either and or but into these sentences so they make sense.**

a I like oranges _____ apples.

b When I go swimming, I take my flippers _____ goggles.

c We can walk by the river _____ we have to be careful.

d Mum is taking me to the cinema _____ we are going to have popcorn.

e We like jam on our toast _____ we don't like butter.

Insert or, but or and in the passage below.

Most octopuses live along the sea bed _____ some species do live near the surface. Octopuses have a rounded body _____ eight arms. These arms have lots of suckers which enable the octopus to taste what it is touching _____ bring food to its mouth. To help avoid predators, an octopus can change colour – to brown, pink, blue _____ green, for example. Octopuses usually live alone _____ make dens by pulling rocks into place.

WILD FACT

To **ESCAPE** from predators, an **OCTOPUS** may **SQUIRT** a cloud of **PURPLE-BLACK INK** before swimming off.

Task 3 Underline the correct joining word in the brackets so that each sentence makes sense.

a Octopuses live in either warm (**and / or / but**) cold waters.

b Octopuses have a skull (**and / or / but**) no skeleton.

c The arms of an octopus have suckers which allow it to grab (**and / or / but**) taste things.

d You would think that an octopus's arms would get tangled up (**and / or / but**) they don't!

Now glide to pages 118–119 to record what you have learned in your Explorer's Logbook.

Joining clauses

You can use the words **when**, **if**, **until** and **because** to join two clauses, depending on what you are trying to say. For example:

*The photographers went out in the boat **because** they wanted to see some whales.*

*Our teacher told us to come inside **if** it started to rain.*

*We cheered the dancers **when** the performance was over.*

*The room was quiet **until** the children came in.*

FACT FILE

Animal:	Orca
I live in:	Coastal waters and open ocean
I eat:	Other types of dolphin, seals, sea lions and fish
I weigh:	Up to 5400 kg!

Task 1 Use when, if, until or because to complete these sentences.

a Orcas are spectacular creatures _____ they sometimes jump completely out of the water.

b The orca grew and grew _____ it became the biggest orca in the ocean.

c I shouted out loud _____ I spotted the orca.

d We decided to take a video _____ we saw an orca.

Task 2 Underline the joining word in brackets that makes most sense.

a Orcas are easy to spot (**because** / **until**) they are black and white and have a large dorsal fin.

b We had never seen orcas so big (**because** / **until**) we went on our trip.

c We wouldn't have gone on the expedition (**if** / **until**) we had known the waves would be so high.

d Orcas use high-pitched clicks (**until** / **when**) they talk to each other.

WILD FACT

ORCAS use **ECHOLOCATION** (sound waves that can travel in water) to **FIND THEIR PREY.**

Task 3 Draw a line from each clause on the left to a clause on the right starting with **when**, **because** or **if** to make a sentence that makes sense.

a We don't know the total number of orcas in the sea

when they hunt baby seals near the water's edge.

b Sea life will benefit

because it is impossible to count them all.

c Orcas will sometimes slide on to a beach

if we reduce the amount of waste entering the ocean.

WILD FACT

ORCAS **TALK** to each other with **SCREAMS, CLICKS AND WHISTLES** or by **SLAPPING THEIR FLIPPERS.**

Now dart to pages 118–119 to record what you have learned in your Explorer's Logbook.

Word classes

Nouns are naming words for objects, people and animals.

The _girl_ walked her _dog_. The _book_ is on the _table_.

Adjectives are describing words.

I am _happy_. The cat is _furry_.

Verbs are doing or being words.

She _drinks_ water every day.
Sam _walked_ to school.

Adverbs give more information about a verb. They often end in **ly**.

I wrote my name _quickly_. She sang _loudly_.

Task 1

Complete the table by writing each word in the correct column. Some examples have been done for you.

swiftly shark look
slowly explorer tightly
binoculars dangerous
sharp hold catch
vicious

Word class			
Noun	**Adjective**	**Verb**	**Adverb**
mouth	_huge_	_eat_	_hungrily_

Task 2 Decide whether each word in bold in the sentences is an **adjective**, an **adverb**, a **verb** or a **noun**, then write your answer on the line.

a The shark **quickly** dived to the sea bed.

_____

b Basking sharks **swim** close to the water's surface.

_____

c **Tiny** plankton are the basking shark's main food.

_____

d Basking sharks like to stay close to the **shore**.

_____

Task 3 Hunt for these nouns, adjectives, adverbs and verbs in the wordsearch. The first letter is in red to help you.

blue

dangerous

breathe

eat

y	c	l	e	v	e	r	l	y	f
q	u	s	a	e	x	y	q	a	i
j	e	s	t	h	p	l	a	e	s
a	r	i	u	i	l	t	g	n	h
f	l	e	s	l	o	w	l	y	a
d	a	n	g	e	r	o	u	s	p
i	u	u	h	i	e	u	l	b	p
n	i	f	x	t	r	y	a	t	i
r	b	r	e	a	t	h	e	p	l
c	a	u	t	i	o	u	s	l	y

explorer

cautiously

cleverly

happily

slowly

fin

fish

sea

Now sweep to pages 118–119 to record what you have learned in your Explorer's Logbook.

Verbs: present tense

The **tense** of a verb shows when things are being done. When you are talking about something that is happening *now*, you should use the **present tense**. There are two ways of writing the present tense:

I **read** my book every day. (= something I often do)

I **am reading** about the box jellyfish. (= something I am doing now)

FACT FILE

Animal:	Box jellyfish
I live in:	Open ocean and coastal water in the western Pacific
I eat:	Fish and shrimp
I weigh:	Up to 2 kg

Task 1 Circle the correct verb form in each sentence.

a At the moment, I (**play** / **am playing**) tennis.

b My friend (**likes** / **is liking**) chocolate.

c Our parents (**enjoy** / **are enjoying**) their holiday.

d I (**brush** / **am brushing**) my teeth every morning.

WILD FACT

A BOX JELLYFISH'S TENTACLES can reach UP TO 3M to stun or kill its prey.

98

Choose the correct verb form from the choices in the brackets to complete each sentence.

a A box jellyfish _____ quite fast. (**swim** / **is swimming** / **swims**)

b A box jellyfish _____ about 15 tentacles. (**is having** / **have** / **has**)

c A box jellyfish _____ its prey. (**is stinging** / **stings** / **sting**)

d The body of the box jellyfish _____ shaped like a cube. (**is being** / **are** / **is**)

WILD FACT

The **BOX JELLYFISH** gets its name from the **CUBE-LIKE SHAPE** of its **BODY.**

Task 3 Solve the crossword, using the verb clues.

Across

1. I do this to my teeth and hair.

5. I do this with a ball.

6. I do this in the playground.

Down

2. I do this with my book.

3. I do this in my bed.

4. I do this in the sea.

5. I do this after I've made a mess!

Now float to pages 118–119 to record what you have learned in your Explorer's Logbook.

Verbs: past tense

WILD FACT

SEA OTTERS float together in GROUPS called RAFTS. They WRAP THEMSELVES in SEA KELP (seaweed) so that they don't drift out too far.

When you talk about something that has already happened, you should use the past tense. Here are two ways of writing the past tense:

*Yesterday, we **walked** to the park.*

*Yesterday, while we **were walking** to the park, my dad fell over.*

Task 1   Underline the correct form of the past tense in brackets in the following sentences.

a Yesterday, we (**visited** / **was visiting**) the aquarium.

b The sea otters (**was floating** / **were floating**) on the water.

c We (**saw** / **was seeing**) sea otters eating small shellfish and fish.

d The explorers (**were filming** / **has filmed**) a raft of sea otters.

Task 2 Write these present tense sentences in the past tense.

a I am watching sea otters on the television.

_____

b I like the programme about sea otters very much!

_____

c There is a great book about sea creatures on on the table.

_____

d We are writing about our aquarium trip.

_____

Task 3 Write 'present tense' or 'past tense' on the line for each of the verbs in bold in these sentences.

a Sea otters **are** carnivores.

_____

b We **saw** a sea otter floating on its back.

_____

c The sea otter **was eating** a fish.

_____

d Sea otters **smash** shellfish on rocks.

_____

e The sea otters **are looking** for food.

_____

Now swim to pages 118–119 to record what you have learned in your Explorer's Logbook.

Expanded noun phrases

FACT FILE

Animal:	Hawksbill turtle
I live in:	Tropical and subtropical coastal water, especially reefs
I eat:	Jellyfish, molluscs, fish and sponges
I weigh:	Up to 68 kg

When you want to give the reader more information about a noun, you can use an expanded noun phrase. You can do this by adding an adjective to describe the noun.

Remember, adjectives are describing words.

a cat → a **ginger** cat
the sky → the **cloudy** sky

A ginger cat and the cloudy sky are expanded noun phrases: ginger describes the cat and cloudy describes the sky.

WILD FACT

HAWKSBILL TURTLES are named after their **NARROW, POINTED BEAK** – it looks similar to a **HAWK'S BEAK!**

Task 1 Underline the expanded noun phrase in each sentence. Look for something that is being described. The first one has been done for you.

Turtles have <u>a bony shell</u>.

a Many species live in the beautiful coral reef.

b The transparent jellyfish swam through the water.

c We are studying interesting sea creatures at school.

Task 2 Choose adjectives to complete the passage below so that it contains expanded noun phrases.

hungry	white	frothy	female	sandy

We stood on the _____ beach to watch the

_____ sea turtles laying eggs. There were

_____, _____ waves, which may have been a

sign of _____ predators.

WILD FACT

MALE SEA TURTLES NEVER LEAVE THE SEA, but FEMALES come ashore to LAY EGGS – to the SAME BEACH where they were HATCHED themselves!

Task 3 Make expanded noun phrases from each noun. Here are some adjectives to help you. The first one has been done for you.

salty	frothy	sharp	scaly	hard	silvery	puffy	huge

Noun	Expanded noun phrase
oyster	the silvery oyster
ocean	
orcas	
puffer fish	

Now crawl to pages 118–119 to record what you have learned in your Explorer's Logbook.

Commas in lists

When you are writing a list of things, you need a **comma** to separate each item. For example:

Mum and I bought apples, oranges, pears and bananas.

It is not usual to put a comma before the word *and*.

FACT FILE

Animal:	Steller sea lion
I live in:	The Pacific Ocean
I eat:	Squid, octopus and fish
I weigh:	Up to 1120 kg

Task 1   Insert the missing commas in the following sentences.

a The explorers put their notebooks pens binoculars and magnifying glasses into their backpacks.

b Our teacher gave us rulers pencils sharpeners and rubbers for the test.

c We bought cheese bread butter and milk from the shop.

d There were swings roundabouts slides and a see-saw in the park.

Task 2 Insert the missing commas in this short passage about sea lions.

We went to look at the Steller sea lions. They have ear flaps long fore-flippers and short hair. We saw bulls cows and pups on some rocks. They were eating squid octopus and fish. It was a long journey back to our hotel. We had to take a helicopter a train a bus and a taxi.

WILD FACT

A **MALE SEA LION** is called a **BULL**, a **FEMALE** is a **COW** and a **BABY** is a **PUP**.

Task 3 Write a list of at least three things you would want for each of these events.

Where you would go	Items you would take
On an adventure	I would take
The park on a snowy day	I would take
On holiday	I would take
A birthday party	I would take

Now wobble your way to pages 118–119 to record what you have learned in your Explorer's Logbook.

Apostrophes

Sometimes you can make words shorter by taking away a letter or letters. Use an **apostrophe** to show where the missing letters would be. For example:

We are getting cold out here. → *We're getting cold out here.*

We're is the shortened form of *we are*. The missing letter is **a**. It is very important to put the apostrophe in the correct place – exactly above where the missing letter or letters should be.

FACT FILE

Animal:	Beluga whale
I live in:	The Arctic Ocean
I eat:	Fish, shellfish and worms
I weigh:	Up to 1350 kg

Task 1

Draw lines to match the words on the top row to their shortened form on the bottom row.

 there is

 I will

 do not

 they have

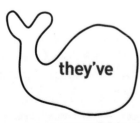 they've

 don't

 I'll

 there's

106

Task 2 Rewrite the words on the left as one shorter word, using an apostrophe.

a I have ⟶ [ ]

b she is ⟶ [ ]

c they had ⟶ [ ]

d you are ⟶ [ ]

WILD FACT

BELUGAS can **SWIM BACKWARDS!**

WILD FACT

The **BELUGA WHALE** can **CHANGE** the **SHAPE** of its **FOREHEAD**, which is called a **MELON!**

Task 3 Rewrite each sentence on the lines below, turning the words shown in bold into one word, using an apostrophe.

a **We have** been learning about beluga whales in class.

_____

b **There is** a nature programme about whales on TV tonight.

_____

c **I am** going to watch it with my dad.

_____

d **He has** already said that I can stay up late!

_____

Now move to pages 118–119 to record what you have learned in your Explorer's Logbook.

Apostrophes to show belonging

When you want to show that something belongs to someone, you can use an **apostrophe**. For example:

My sister's coat is on the peg.
(the coat belongs to my sister)

Sam has lost his dog's collar.
(the collar belongs to the dog)

It is very important that you put the apostrophe in the correct place, between the last letter of the word and the letter 's'.

FACT FILE

Animal:	Stingray
I live in:	Coastal water, but occasionally in open ocean
I eat:	Crabs, clams, oysters and sea snails
I weigh:	Up to 350 kg

Task 1 Insert the missing apostrophe in the correct place in each sentence.

a An oceanic manta rays wingspan is up to 7 metres.

b Our teachers husband saw a stingray on holiday.

c He was going to take a photograph with his cousins camera.

d Unfortunately, he had left it at his friends house.

Task 2

Change the phrases on the left so that they use an apostrophe to show that something belongs to someone. Write the new phrase on the line. The first one has been done for you.

a   the pen belonging to my sister   <u>my sister's pen</u>

b   the ball belonging to Liam   _____

c   the bowl belonging to the dog   _____

d   the charts belonging to the sailor   _____

WILD FACT

To swim, a **STINGRAY** moves its body with a **WAVE-LIKE** motion or **FLAPS ITS FINS.**

WILD FACT

STINGRAYS use a **VENOMOUS STINGER** on their **TAIL** to **DEFEND** themselves.

Task 3

Add an apostrophe and the letter 's' to the words in the box and then complete the sentences.

stingray	class	Saira	boat

a   The _____ eyes are on the top of its head, but its mouth is on the lower side.

b   Our _____ new topic is sea creatures.

c   _____ picture of a stingray has been put on the wall.

d   The _____ engine has broken.

Now coast to pages 118–119 to record what you have learned in your Explorer's Logbook.

Quick quiz

Now try these questions. Give yourself 1 mark for every correct answer.

1   **Insert the missing apostrophes to show *belonging* in this sentence.**

My brothers teddy is on my sisters bed.

2   **Change the present tense verbs in brackets into the past tense. Write the past tense verb on the line.**

   a I (eat) _____ my breakfast at 8 o'clock.

   b My mum (makes) _____ me wipe my feet.

3   **Write the words in *bold* as one word by using an apostrophe to replace missing letters.**

I (**could not**) _____ believe that they (**did not**)

_____ win the match after (**they had**) _____

practised so hard.

4   **Insert either *and*, *or*, or *but* in these sentences.**

I enjoy English _____ not maths. I like both art _____ PE.

We can choose a story _____ a film on the last day of term.

5   **Write these sentences correctly, using the correct punctuation.**

   a look at the electric eels _____

   b there are so many _____

   c have you seen the sharks _____

6   **Tick a box in each row to show whether each word is an adjective, a noun, a verb or an adverb.**

Word	Adjective	Noun	Verb	Adverb
eat				
swiftly				
fin				
shiny				

7 **Insert the missing commas in this sentence.** ☐

I am going to take a notebook a waterproof coat a camera and some binoculars on my whale-watching trip.

8 **Underline the *two* expanded noun phrases in this sentence.** ☐

We all thought that the venomous stingray was the best creature.

9 **Rewrite this sentence using correct punctuation.** ☐

my brother and i went to scotland in the summer

_____

_____

10 **Use *when*, *if*, *until* or *because* to join these clauses.**

a I go to bed _____ I've brushed my teeth. ☐

b I have porridge for breakfast _____ it is healthy. ☐

c I also have toast _____ I am very hungry. ☐

d I watch TV _____ it is time to go. ☐

11 **Change these verbs from the past tense into the present tense as if you are carrying out the action.** ☐

Example: ran *I run / I am running*_____

swam _____

did _____

12 **Underline the word in this sentence that tells you it is a command.** ☐

Finish your homework quickly.

13 **Write down the verbs in these sentences and then change them from the present tense to the past tense.**

a I am reading my book.

Verb: _____   Past tense: _____ ☐

b Milo and Jack are jumping into the pool.

Verb: _____   Past tense: _____ ☐

How did you do? | 1–5 Try again! | 6–10 Good try!

11–15 Great work! | 16–20 Excellent exploring!

/20

111

Explorer's Logbook

Maths: Ages 5–6

Tick off the topics as you complete them and colour in the star to show how you feel.

How do you feel?
- Needs practice
- Nearly there
- Got it!

Place value ☐

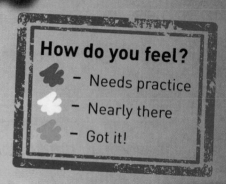

Ordering numbers ☐

More ordering numbers ☐

Writing numbers ☐

Multiplication ☐

Division ☐

Checking your maths ☐

Fractions ☐

Measuring ☐

Understanding time ☐

2D and 3D shapes ☐

Money ☐

Explorer's Logbook

Maths: Ages 6–7

Tick off the topics as you complete them and colour in the star to show how you feel.

How do you feel?
- Needs practice
- Nearly there
- Got it!

Counting ☐

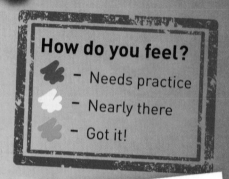

Compare and order numbers ☐

Add numbers ☐

Subtract numbers ☐

Multiply and divide ☐

Fractions ☐

Measure ☐

Money ☐

Time ☐

2D shapes ☐

3D shapes ☐

Statistics ☐

Explorer's Logbook

Phonics and Spelling: Ages 5-7

Tick off the topics as you complete them and colour in the star to show how you feel.

Consonants and vowels ☐

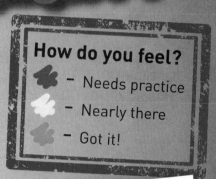

Phonics and decodable words ☐

Double letters at the end of words ☐

Word endings ve and y ☐

Adding s or es to nouns and verbs ☐

Adding ing or ed to verbs ☐

The graphemes ie, i-e, igh, y, oy and oi ☐

Using double vowel digraphs ☐

The phoneme s ☐

Silent letters ☐

er and est ☐

Homophones ☐

Explorer's Logbook

Grammar and Punctuation: Ages 5–7

Tick off the topics as you complete them and colour in the star to show how you feel.

How do you feel?
- Needs practice
- Nearly there
- Got it!

Capital letters ☐

Exclamations and commands ☐

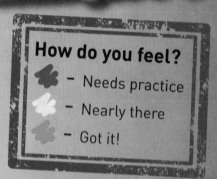

Statements and questions ☐

And, or, but ☐

Joining clauses ☐

Word classes ☐

Verbs: present tense ☐

Verbs: past tense ☐

Expanded noun phrases ☐

Commas in lists ☐

Apostrophes ☐

Apostrophes to
show belonging ☐

Answers Maths Ages 5–6

Pages 8–9

Task 1

a 23 b 35 c 42

Task 2

a Any number that uses any two of the available digits, e.g. 12, 31, 43, 24

b 43

c 12

Task 3

a 6 b 20 c 7

d 70 e 40 f 90

Pages 10–11

Task 1

a 3, 5 b 5, 7 c 8, 10

Task 2

a 15 b 30 c 23 d 14

Task 3

One less		One more
55	56	57
33	34	35
20	21	22
1	2	3
12	13	14
72	73	74
54	55	56

Pages 12–13

Task 1

a 3, 12, 14, 26, 32

b 2, 7, 13, 29, 45

c 3, 16, 21, 23, 60

d 10, 13, 43, 51, 54

Task 2

a 10, 8, 6, 3, 2

b 34, 20, 18, 16, 4

c 51, 39, 27, 16, 5

Task 3

12, 14, 16, 18, 20 ✓

Task 4

2 **3** 4 **5** 6 **7**

Pages 14–15

Task 1

a eight b six c twelve d three

Task 2

a 5 b 20 c 11 d 1

Task 3

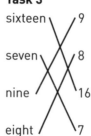

Task 4

a seven b fourteen

c twenty-one d forty-three

Pages 16–17

Task 1

a $5 + 5 + 5$ **or** $3 + 3 + 3 + 3 + 3$

b $10 + 10 + 10 + 10 + 10$ **or** $5 + 5 + 5 + 5 + 5 + 5 + 5 + 5 + 5 + 5$

c $2 + 2 + 2 + 2 + 2 + 2$ **or** $6 + 6$

Task 2

a 10×5 **or** 5×10

b 2×7 **or** 7×2

c 5×7 **or** 7×5

Task 3

a 10 b 60 c 16

Task 4

a $3 \times 5 = 15$ b $6 \times 2 = 12$

c $4 \times 4 = 16$ d $6 \times 3 = 18$

Pages 18–19

Task 1

a $2 \div 2 = 1$ b $4 \div 2 = 2$

c $12 \div 2 = 6$ d $14 \div 2 = 7$

Task 2

$10 \div 2 = 5$

Task 3

a 2 b 3 c 6

Pages 20–21

Task 1

a $3 - 1 = 2$

b $7 - 1 = 6$

c $10 - 6 = 4$

Task 2

a $6 \div 2 = 3$ b $8 \div 2 = 4$

c $12 \div 2 = 6$ d $20 \div 10 = 2$

Task 3

a $12 - 10 = 2$ b $5 \times 2 = 10$ c $10 + 10 = 20$

Pages 22–23

Task 1

a   b

Task 2

a 3 b 4 c 5

Task 3

a 1   **b** 2   **c** 3

Pages 24–25

Task 1

Giraffe A is taller

Task 2

a Giraffe A eats 3 kg, giraffe B eats 4 kg

b Giraffe B

Task 3

a Giraffe A drank 9 litres, giraffe B drank 7 litres

b Giraffe B

Pages 26–27

Task 1

 a   **b**   **c**

Task 2

 a   **b**   **c**

Task 3

a 8 weeks

b 1 month = 4 weeks, so 2 months = 2 × 4 = 8 weeks

Pages 28–29

Task 1

Square — Triangle

Triangle — Square

Circle — Rectangle

Rectangle — Circle

Task 2

a cuboid   **b** cylinder

c cone   **d** pyramid

Task 3

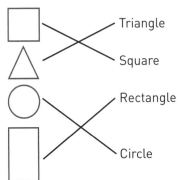

	2D	3D
triangle	✓	
cylinder		✓
octagon	✓	
cube		✓

Pages 30–31

Task 1

a 6p   **b** 10p   **c** 12p

Task 2

Any combination of available coins, e.g. 10 × 1p, 2 × 5p, 5p + 2p + 2p + 1p

Task 3

a 20p, 50p, £1, £2

b 5

c 5

Pages 32–33

1 3, 5, 7, 12, 14

2 19

3 10

4 5 × 4 **or** 4 × 5

5 2 + 2 + 2 + 2 **or** 4 + 4

6 5

7 10 – 4 = 6

8 5 + 7 = 12

9 3 hyenas

10 2

11 5 hours

12 1 kg, 3 kg, 10 kg, 12 kg

13

14 D

15 cuboid

16 ✓

17 It has no straight sides/edges

18 10p

19 2p

20 17p

Pages 34–35

Task 1

a 2, 4, 6, 8, 10   b 3, 6, 9, 12,15

c 5, 10, 15, 20, 25

Task 2

a 45, 50, 55, **60**, 65, **70**   b 24, 21, 18, **15**, 12, 9, **6**

c 52, 62, **72**, 82, **92**   d 78, **68**, 58, **48**, 38, 28

Task 3

a 63, 73, 83   b 75, 85, 95   c 32, 42, 52

Pages 36–37

Task 1

a 1, 2, 5, 7, 8, 9   b 3, 6, 14, 16, 24, 26

c 45, 47, 54, 56, 65, 74

Task 2

a <   b >   c <

Task 3

a 34 < 78   b 12 = 6 + 6   c 29 < 46

d 87 > 57   e 9 + 9 = 18   f 1 > 0

Pages 38–39

Task 1

a 5 + 3 = 8   b 6 + 7 = 13

Task 2

a 21   b 57   c 16

Task 3

69

Pages 40–41

Task 1

a 10 − 7 = 3, 10 − 3 = 7

b 20 − 5 = 15, 20 − 15 = 5

c 20 − 2 = 18, 20 − 18 = 2

Task 2

a 32 − 9 = **23**   b 78 − 30 = **48**

c 64 − 31 = **33**   d 83 − 46 = **37**

Task 3

a 18 − **12** = 6   b **28** − 5 = 23

c 45 − **6** = 39   d **48** − 30 = 18

Pages 42–43

Task 1

a ◯◯ 2 × 4 = 8   b ◯◯◯◯ 4 × 3 = 12
   ◯◯   ◯◯◯◯
   ◯◯   ◯◯◯◯
   ◯◯

c ◯◯◯◯◯◯ 6 × 2 = 12
   ◯◯◯◯◯◯

Task 2

a 3 × 5 = 15, 5 × 3 = 15, 15 ÷ 3 = 5, 15 ÷ 5 = 3

b 2 × 6 = 12, 6 × 2 = 12, 12 ÷ 6 = 2, 12 ÷ 2 = 6

Task 3

a 20   b 21

Pages 44–45

Task 1

a $\frac{1}{2}$ b $\frac{1}{4}$ c $\frac{1}{3}$

d $\frac{2}{4}$ or $\frac{1}{2}$ e $\frac{3}{4}$ f $\frac{2}{4}$ or $\frac{1}{2}$

Task 2

Task 3

a $\frac{3}{4}$ = 3 eggs   b $\frac{1}{2}$ = 4 eggs

c $\frac{1}{4}$ = 3 eggs   d $\frac{1}{3}$ = 2 eggs

Pages 46–47

Task 1

kilograms   millimetres   metres   grams   millilitres   degrees

centimetres   centimetres   litres

Task 2

a holds more than   b is shorter than

c is heavier than   d is shorter than

e is more than   f is heavier than

Task 3

Water boils at a temperature of	10°C	(100°C)	1°C	1000°C
An apple weighs	10 kg	1 kg	(100 g)	1000 kg
A teaspoon holds	(5 ml)	50 l	500 l	5 l
The length of a pencil is	10 m	1 m	1 mm	(10 cm)

Pages 48–49

Task 1

a 18p   b 36p   c 57p

Task 2

a 10p, 5p, 2 × 2p or equivalents

b 20p, 10p, 2 × 2p or equivalents

c 50p, 20p, 10p, 5p, 2p, 1p or equivalents

Task 3

a 14p   b 76p   c £1.50 or 150p

Pages 50–51

Task 1

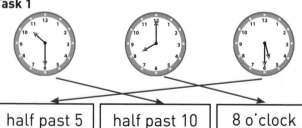

| half past 5 | half past 10 | 8 o'clock |

Task 2

a quarter past 10 (or 10.15) **b** half past 8 (or 8.30)
c quarter to 5 (or 4.45)

Task 3

a 25 past 10 (or 10.25) **b** 5 to 8 (or 7.55)
c 10 past 5 (or 5.10) **d** 20 to 12 (or 11.40)

Pages 52–53

Task 1

a 0 **b** 3 **c** 4 **d** 4 **e** 5 **f** 6 **g** 8

Task 2

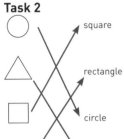
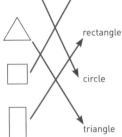

Task 3

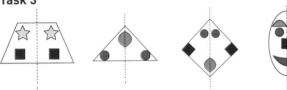

Pages 54–55

Task 1

cube, 8 vertices, 6 faces, 12 edges

Task 2

Shapes with straight edges	Shapes with curved edges
cube	cylinder
cuboid	cone
square pyramid	
triangular prism	
tetrahedron	

Task 3

a 6 squares **b** 2 circles and a rectangle
c 3 rectangles and 2 triangles

Pages 56–57

Task 1

a

	Number of katydids	Total
Adam	ⅢⅠ ⅠⅠⅠⅠ	9
Zeikel	ⅠⅠⅠⅠ	4
Joel	ⅢⅠ ⅢⅠ Ⅰ	11
Meera	ⅢⅠ ⅠⅠⅠ	8

b Joel (11) **c** Zeikel (4)

Task 2

a Thursday **b** 15 mm **c** Wednesday and Friday

d

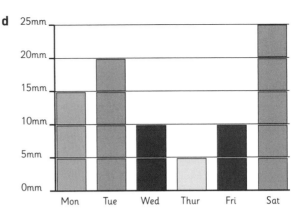

Task 3

a Trees 9, Grass 12, Leaves 11, Logs 8
b 40

Pages 58–59

1 a 10, 12, 14 **b** 13, 16, 19 **c** 10, 5, 0
2 3, 12, 27, 46, 58, 84
3 a 18 **b** 22
4 a 38 **b** 25
5 a 14 **b** 5
6

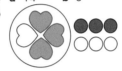

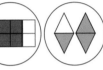

7 2 ladybirds shaded
8 6 cm
9

Length	Mass	Capacity
centimetres	grams	litres
metres	kilograms	millilitres
kilometres		
millimetres		

10 38p
11 a 4 o'clock **b** half past 2 (or 2.30)
    c 10 to 3 (or 2.50) **d** half past 12 (or 12.30)
12

rectangle sphere triangle cylinder cube cuboid square pyramid

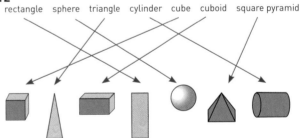

Answers Phonics and Spelling Ages 5-7

Pages 60–61

Task 1

a fox / fix **b** tub / tab **c** kid **d** lid / lad / led
e can / con **f** rag / rig / rug **g** yes **h** jam
i wet / wit **j** zip / zap

Task 2

a chop / chip / chap **b** flat / flit
c spin / spun / span **d** grab / grub
e swim / swam / swum **f** trap / trip
g drag / dreg / drug **h** shed / shod
i plan **j** that
k slit / slat / slot **l** trim / tram

Task 3

a lets / lots **b** much **c** sing / sang / sung / song
d neck / nick **e** band / bend / bond / bind
f camp **g** want / went **h** vest / vast
i gift **j** bulb **k** link **l** kept

Task 4

a The d**e**nt**i**st looks after your teeth.
b The r**o**ck**e**t went up to the moon.
c A r**o**b**i**n is a bird that lives in the garden.
d At Halloween we use a p**u**mpk**i**n to make a lantern.

Pages 62–63

Task 1

a trunk **b** grab **c** shop **d** thing

Task 2

a take, flop, bake **b** jam, week, twin
c soggy, flow **d** chop, kill, silk

Task 3

Any combination of consonants and vowels

Task 4

	Consonant blend	Digraph	Trigraph
such		✓	
catch			✓
stay	✓		
hedge			✓
shut		✓	
duck		✓	

Pages 64–65

Task 1

Two from peacock, peachick, black, neck

Task 2

a thick **b** black **c** sock **d** peck
e shock **f** flick **g** muck **h** quack

Task 3

a jazz **b** dress **c** pull / puff / puss
d mess **e** bull / buzz / buff **f** cliff
g chess **h** mill / miss / miff

Task 4

a I found a **shell** on the beach.
b I love to **kick** a **ball**.
c My hat blew **off** in the wind.
d I like to hear the bees **buzz**.
e My brother made such a **fuss** when he **fell** down.

Pages 66–67

Task 1

a My dad has a **shave** every day.
b I **love** watching the orangutans play.

c When I go home, I **wave** goodbye to my friends.
d My arm slides into my **sleeve**.
e There are **twelve** eggs in the box.
f I **have** a drink of milk before I go to bed.

Task 2

a Any rhyming word, e.g. cave, brave, Dave, crave, grave, nave, rave, slave, wave
b Any rhyming word, e.g. alive, dive, drive, hive, jive, live
c Any rhyming word, e.g. above, dove, glove
d Any rhyming word, e.g. live, sieve
e Any rhyming word, e.g. believe, grieve, heave, sleeve, Steve, weave

Task 3

Words with a 'y' ending that sounds like 'eye'	Words with a 'y' ending that sounds like 'ee'
try	very
fly	merry
spy	fairy
cry	happy
fry	puppy
why	silly
shy	candy
my	windy
by	mummy

Pages 68–69

Task 1

a cat**s**, witch**es**, banana**s**, fox**es**, brush**es**
b dog**s**, window**s**, church**es**, chip**s**, kiss**es**
c bus**es**, toy**s**, lad**s**, cliff**s**, dish**es**
d animal**s**, duck**s**, pill**s**, cow**s**, class**es**

Task 2

a glasses **b** brooms **c** watches **d** sixes
e lunches **f** dolphins **g** apples **h** bushes
i pegs **j** trucks

Task 3

a Millie **runs** to see the fruit bat.
b Sam **shows** his picture to his mum.
c The snake **hisses** loudly.
d Fred **rings** the doorbell.
e Dad **fixes** the lock on the box.
f Mum **fills** my glass with water.

Pages 70–71

Task 1

a injecting, injected **b** staying, stayed
c weighing, weighed

Task 2

a hunting, hunted **b** pinching, pinched
c crawling, crawled

Task 3

Any words that can have **ing** and **ed** added without altering the root word

Task 4

a sang **b** thing **c** gong **d** bring
e hung **f** belong **g** ring **h** lung
i king **j** fang **k** rung **l** pong

Pages 72–73

Task 1

raccoon, food, bamboo, shoots

Task 2
a moon, soon   **b** hoop, loop
c zoom, boom   **d** food, mood

Task 3
Any two from: feet, trees, seen

Task 4
a week   **b** keep   **c** meet   **d** weed   **e** heel

Pages 74–75
Task 1
a Any two words that rhyme, e.g. joy, toy, enjoy, annoy
b Any two words that rhyme, e.g. oil, foil, boil, soil, toil
c Any two words that rhyme, e.g. coin, join

Task 2
a I have a sore throat and I have lost my **voice**.
b I like to **join** in with all the games.
c I planted a seed in the **soil**.
d The referee tossed a **coin** to see who would start.
e I found my car in the **toy** box.
f Stop cheating! You will **spoil** the game!

Task 3
a It was dark, so I put on the **light**.
b When I **lie** in bed, I turn on my **side**.
c I **bite** on my apple.
d My brother upset me and made me **cry**.
e I **tie** the string in a **tight** knot.
f I **like** to **fly my kite**.

Pages 76–77
Task 1
a Any three words that rhyme, e.g. face, lace, pace, race, trace
b Any two words that rhyme, e.g. dice, lice, mice, nice, price, rice, slice, twice

Task 2
bicycle, juicy, lacy, Lucy, mercy, icicle, prince, city, voice, dance, circle, circus

Task 3
Across: 2 race, **4** space, **5** fancy, **Down: 1** France, **3** spice

Pages 78–79
Task 1
a My <u>knees</u> began to <u>knock</u> when I saw the tiger.
b Jack said he had seen a <u>ghost</u>.
c I <u>know</u> that Tom got it <u>wrong</u>.
d Asif tried to <u>guess</u> the song I played on the <u>guitar</u>.
e Daisy cut her <u>thumb</u> while <u>knitting</u>.
f Rowan fell down and broke his <u>wrist</u>.

Task 2
a gnome, wrap   **b** doubt, numb
c column, wring   **d** gnat, guide
e wriggle, crumb

Task 3
a scissors   **b** talk   **c** island
d listen   **e** autumn

Pages 80–81
Task 1
a cool, cooler, coolest   **b** soft, softer, softest
c great, greater, greatest

Task 2
a wise, wiser, wisest   **b** simple, simpler, simplest
c strange, stranger, strangest

Task 3
a red, redder, reddest   **b** sad, sadder, saddest
c hot, hotter, hottest

Task 4
a silly, sillier, silliest   **b** lazy, lazier, laziest
c funny, funnier, funniest

Pages 82–83
Task 1
a The children took **their** dog for a walk.
b Look at that camel over **there**!
c **There** are lots of camels in Asia.
d The dogs wagged **their** tails when they saw **their** owner.

Task 2
a I went to the shops to **buy** an apple.
b I have been waiting all **week** to see a camel.
c The wind **blew** the sand across the desert.

Task 3
a It was much **too** hot in the desert.
b We went **to** see the camels in the zoo.
c Bactrian camels have **two** humps each.

Pages 84–85
1 a smarter, smartest   **b** easier, easiest
   c wetter, wettest   **d** nicer, nicest
2 a brushes   **b** cubs   **c** caves
3 a There are many **deer** roaming in the woods.
   b You are my **dear** friend.
   c I have a **knot** in my shoe lace.
   d A camel's spit is **not** very pleasant!
   e I will **write** a letter to my grandma.
   f I am **right**-handed, but my mum is left-handed.
4 a I adopted a r**a**bb**i**t that needed a n**ew** h**o**me.
   b My d**a**d w**e**nt to the sh**o**ps.
   c The c**u**p of m**i**lk was very h**o**t.
   d I love f**i**sh and ch**i**ps for my dinn**e**r.
5 Any five words, e.g.: batch, botch, catch, hatch, watch, ditch, hitch, witch, hutch, badge, bodge, budge, cadge, hedge, dodge, wedge
6 a e.g. numb, thumb, dumb
   b e.g. knife
   c e.g. wrong
   d e.g. ghost
   e e.g. wrist
7 Any five words, e.g. juice, juicy, voice, nice, grace, pace, once, twice, ice, lice, icy, pencil, icicle, city, cycle, mercy, fancy, mice
8 a bri**ck**   **b** acro**ss**   **c** flu**ff**
   d tri**ck** / tri**ll**   **e** whi**ff** / whi**zz**
   f dre**ss**   **g** hu**ll** / hu**ff**
   h sti**ff** / sti**ck** / sti**ll**   **i** ta**ll** / ta**ck**
9 a Any rhyming word with **oo**, e.g. hoof, goof
   b Any rhyming word with **oo**, e.g. fool, drool, cool, school
   c Any rhyming word with **oo**, e.g. shoot, coot, boot, loot
10 a Any from: bike, by, buy, bite
   b Any from: high, hike, hide
   c Any from: lie, like, light, lime, lice
   d Any from: flight, fly
   e Any from: trike, trice, try, tribe, tripe
   f Any from: shy, shine
11 a I was go**ing** to school when I met a dog.
   b The lady show**ed** me the way to the park.
   c I have always want**ed** a hamster.
   d The fruit bat is fly**ing** in and out of the trees.
   e The scorpion dart**ed** towards the rocks.
   f The python is slither**ing** away.
12 a sky   **b** funny

 **Grammar and Punctuation Ages 5–7**

Pages 86–87
Task 1

	Person's name	Place name	Day of the week	Month of the year
Last <u>Saturday</u>, I went to the aquarium in <u>Manchester</u>.		✓	✓	
Next <u>August</u>, we are going to <u>North America</u>.		✓		✓
<u>Jack</u> saw a film about crabs in <u>London</u>.	✓	✓		

Task 2
a I, July
b Atlanta, United States
Task 3
Last **F**riday, **R**osewood **P**rimary went to **B**lue **P**lanet **A**quarium in **C**hester. **W**e saw all sorts of underwater creatures. **M**rs **S**mith said that we would be starting a project on sea life. **M**y friend **M**arcus and **I** took lots of photographs, which his dad, **M**r **J**ones, is going to print out.

Pages 88–89
Task 1
a A shark can grow to be as big as a bus.
b Do all sharks eat meat?
c There are about 460 species of shark.
d Have you seen my book about sharks?
Task 2

Are there any sharks in Great Britain?	Question
Sharks have rows and rows of teeth.	Statement
Which species of shark is the biggest?	Question
Great white sharks can move at speeds of up to 24 km/h (15 mph).	Statement

Task 3
Answers will vary. Each question to start with a capital letter and end with a question mark.

Pages 90–91
Task 1
a **W**hat an enormous puffer fish!
b **L**ook at that amazing coral!
c **I** can't believe how big that puffer fish can puff itself up!
Task 2
a <u>Watch</u> the puffer fish carefully.
b <u>Take</u> a photograph of it swimming.
c <u>Stick</u> the photograph in your book.
d <u>Write</u> a sentence about it.
Task 3
Answers will vary. Each sentence should contain a command verb and end with a full stop or an exclamation mark, e.g. *Eat those worms. Swim this way. Follow that shark.*

Pages 92–93
Task 1
a I like oranges **and** apples.
b When I go swimming, I take my flippers **and** goggles.
c We can walk by the river **but** we have to be careful.
d Mum is taking me to the cinema **and** we are going to have popcorn.
e We like jam on our toast **but** we don't like butter.
Task 2
Most octopuses live along the sea bed **but** some species do live near the surface. Octopuses have a rounded body **and** eight arms. These arms have lots of suckers which enable the octopus to taste what it is touching **and** bring food to its mouth. To help avoid predators, an octopus can change colour – to brown, pink, blue **or** green, for example. Octopuses usually live alone **and** make dens by pulling rocks into place.
Task 3
a or   b but   c and   d but

Pages 94–95
Task 1
a Orcas are spectacular creatures **because** they sometimes jump completely out of the water.
b The orca grew and grew **until** it became the biggest orca in the ocean.
c I shouted out loud **when** (or **because**) I spotted the orca.
d We decided to take a video **when** (or **because**) we saw an orca.
Task 2
a Orcas are easy to spot **<u>because</u>** they are black and white and have a large dorsal fin.
b We had never seen orcas so big **<u>until</u>** we went on our trip.
c We wouldn't have gone on the expedition **if** we had known the waves would be so high.
d Orcas use high-pitched clicks **<u>when</u>** they talk to each other.
Task 3
a We don't know the total number of orcas in the sea – because it is impossible to count them all.
b Sea life will benefit – if we reduce the amount of waste entering the ocean.
c Orcas will sometimes slide on to a beach – when they hunt baby seals near the water's edge.

Pages 96–97
Task 1

Word class			
Noun	**Adjective**	**Verb**	**Adverb**
mouth	huge	eat	hungrily
shark	sharp	catch	swiftly
binoculars	vicious	hold	slowly
explorer	dangerous	look	tightly

Task 2
a quickly – adverb   b swim – verb
c tiny – adjective   d shore – noun

Task 3

y	c	l	e	v	e	r	l	y	f
q	u	s	a	e	x	y	q	a	i
j	e	s	t	h	p	l	a	e	s
a	r	i	u	i	l	t	g	n	h
f	l	e	s	l	o	w	l	y	a
d	a	n	g	e	r	o	u	s	p
i	u	u	h	i	e	u	l	b	p
n	i	f	x	t	r	y	a	t	i
r	b	r	e	a	t	h	e	p	l
c	a	u	t	i	o	u	s	l	y

Pages 98–99
Task 1
a At the moment, I **am playing** tennis.
b My friend **likes** chocolate.
c Our parents **are enjoying** their holiday.
d I **brush** my teeth every morning.

Task 2
a A box jellyfish **swims / is swimming** quite fast.
b A box jellyfish **has** about 15 tentacles.
c A box jellyfish **stings / is stinging** its prey.
d The body of the box jellyfish **is** shaped like a cube.

Task 3
Across

1 brush   **5** throw   **6** play

Down

2 read   **3** sleep   **4** swim   **5** tidy

Pages 100–101
Task 1
a Yesterday, we **visited** the aquarium.
b The sea otters **were floating** on the water.
c We **saw** sea otters eating small shellfish and fish.
d The explorers **were filming** a raft of sea otters.

Task 2
a I was watching sea otters on the television.
b I liked the programme about sea otters very much!
c There was a great book about sea creatures on the table.
d We were writing about our aquarium trip.

Task 3
a are – present tense   **b** saw – past tense
c was eating – past tense **d** smash – present tense
e are looking – present tense

Pages 102–103
Task 1
a Many species live in the beautiful coral reef.
b The transparent jellyfish swam through the water.
c We are studying interesting sea creatures at school.

Task 2
We stood on the **sandy** beach to watch the **female** sea turtles laying eggs. There were **white**, **frothy** waves, which may have been a sign of **hungry** predators.

Task 3
Answers will vary. Examples:
the salty ocean
the huge orcas
a puffy puffer fish

Pages 104–105
Task 1
a The explorers put their notebooks, pens, binoculars and magnifying glasses into their backpacks.
b Our teacher gave us rulers, pencils, sharpeners and rubbers for the test.
c We bought cheese, bread, butter and milk from the shop.

d There were swings, roundabouts, slides and a see-saw in the park.

Task 2
We went to look at the Steller sea lions. They have ear flaps, long fore-flippers and short hair. We saw bulls, cows and pups on some rocks. They were eating squid, octopus and fish. It was a long journey back to our hotel. We had to take a helicopter, a train, a bus and a taxi.

Task 3
Answers will vary. Lists of items must be separated by commas.

Pages 106–107
Task 1
there is – there's; I will – I'll; do not – don't; they have – they've

Task 2
a I have – I've   **b** she is – she's
c they had – they'd **d** you are – you're

Task 3
a We've been learning about beluga whales in class.
b There's a nature programme about whales on TV tonight.
c I'm going to watch it with my dad.
d He's already said that I can stay up late!

Pages 108–109
Task 1
a An oceanic manta **ray's** wingspan is up to 7 metres.
b Our **teacher's** husband saw a stingray on holiday.
c He was going to take a photograph with his **cousin's** camera.
d Unfortunately, he had left it at his **friend's** house.

Task 2
a my sister's pen   **b** Liam's ball
c the dog's bowl   **d** the sailor's charts

Task 3
a The **stingray's** eyes are on the top of its head, but its mouth is on the lower side.
b Our **class's** new topic is sea creatures.
c **Saira's** picture of a stingray has been put on the wall.
d The **boat's** engine has broken.

Pages 110–111
1 My brother's teddy is on my sister's bed.
2 a ate   **b** made
3 I **couldn't** believe that they **didn't** win the match after **they'd** practised so hard.
4 I enjoy English **but** not maths. I like both art **and** PE. We can choose a story **or** a film on the last day of term.
5 a Look at the electric eels. (or !)
  b There are so many.
  c Have you seen the sharks?
6 eat – verb; swiftly – adverb; fin – noun; shiny – adjective
7 I am going to take a notebook, a waterproof coat, a camera and some binoculars on my whale-watching trip.
8 We all thought that the venomous stingray was the best creature.
9 My brother and I went to Scotland in the summer.
10 a I go to bed **when** I've brushed my teeth.
  b I have porridge for breakfast **because** it is healthy.
  c I have toast **if** (or **when**) I am very hungry.
  d I watch TV **until** it is time to go.
11 I swim / I am swimming; I do / I am doing
12 Finish your homework quickly.
13 a am reading / was reading (**or** read)
  b are jumping / were jumping (**or** jumped)

You're awesome!

Well done, you have finished your adventures!

Explorer's pass

Name: _____

Age: _____

Date: _____

Draw a picture of yourself in the box!